COGNITIVE
VIEWS
OF
HUMAN
MOTIVATION

COGNITIVE VIEWS OF HUMAN MOTIVATION

Edited by

BERNARD WEINER

University of California, Los Angeles

ACADEMIC PRESS, INC.

New York   San Francisco   London

A Subsidiary of Harcourt Brace Jovanovich, Publishers

ACADEMIC PRESS, INC.
111 Fifth Avenue, New York, New York 10003

United Kingdom Edition published by
ACADEMIC PRESS, INC. (LONDON) LTD.
24/28 Oval Road, London NW1

LIBRARY OF CONGRESS CATALOG CARD NUMBER: 74-27385

ISBN 0-12-741950-0

PRINTED IN THE UNITED STATES OF AMERICA

CONTENTS

v

CONTRIBUTORS

John W. Atkinson,
   Department of Psychology, University of Michigan, Ann Arbor, Michigan 48104

David Birch
   Department of Psychology, University of Michigan, Ann Arbor, Michigan 48104

Robert C. Bolles
   Department of Psychology, University of Washington, Seattle, Washington 98195

Kenneth Bongort
   Department of Psychology, University of Michigan, Ann Arbor, Michigan 48104

Richard S. Lazarus
   Department of Psychology, University of California, Berkeley, Berkeley, California 94720

Walter Mischel
   Department of Psychology, Stanford University, Stanford, California 94305

Robert R. Sears
Department of Psychology, Stanford University, Stanford, California 94305

Bernard Weiner
Department of Psychology, University of California, Los Angeles, Los Angeles, California 90024

PREFACE

The papers in this volume were first presented during a symposium at the annual convention of the American Association for the Advancement of Science (AAAS), held in San Francisco in February, 1974. The symposium was organized at the request of the AAAS Psychology section, headed by Dr. William Garvey, and with the encouragement of Dr. Charles Cofer, a member of the AAAS Psychology committee.

Planning a symposium that was pre-titled "Cognitive Views of Human Motivation" posed many difficulties. I first had to decide what topics should be represented. It was tempting to invite speakers identified with one particular area of study, such as achievement motivation, cognitive balance, defense mechanisms, and so on. A communality of interests certainly facilitates communication. On the other hand, a wide scope of cognitive and motivational processes could have been examined, ranging from a molecular analysis of, for example, information processing, to the molar study of self-actualization tendencies or the effects of political ideology on behavior.

After considerable deliberation it was decided to follow a middle course and to include a moderate range of topics. I hoped to select phenomena that had been studied objectively without reducing their meaning or impoverishing their practical significance. Such a compromise runs the risk of satisfying no one and doubts were raised by some of the symposium participants.

After determining the general scope of the symposium, the participants had to be selected. Here again difficult decisions were faced. Young and promising psychologists in the field could have been brought together, for they are most likely to be influenced by scientific interchange. However, a symposium of younger and lesser-known participants is not best in the setting of a AAAS convention. The AAAS was founded by natural scientists. Even with the later inclusion of the social sciences, the psychological symposia have been dominated by "hard" areas, such as physiological psychology and learning. I therefore felt that established scientists had to be invited to this apparently "soft" symposium, even though their personal research activities might be little affected by the exchange of ideas. It was too important and unique an invitation to risk on anyone but proven scholars!

In the field of motivation there are many qualified psychologists. Some of my conflicts about selection were resolved by opting for theoretical diversity. I decided to invite a representative from ego psychology, someone with behavioristic training, a social learning theorist, an individual primarily influenced by Lewin or Tolman, and so on. In this manner the listeners and readers could become aware of the diversity of cognitive approaches and gain familiarity with a variety of areas of research. Finally, I wanted to enclose invited research addresses between an introduction by someone with historical perspective and a discussion by someone with analytic skills and wide experience.

Fortunately, outstanding individuals were available who responded positively to my call. Robert C. Bolles, the someone with historical perspective, agreed to write an introduction. David Birch and John W. Atkinson, Richard S. Lazarus, and Walter Mischel, major contributors to the field with contrasting theoretical orientations, consented to give research addresses. I did not want to be left out and took the liberty of also inviting myself to fill this role. And Robert R. Sears, known for his analytical skills and great breadth of experience, accepted the task of the discussant. Dr. Sears was so provocative that some of the research contributors decided to add a concluding statement, responding to some of the challenges raised in the discussion. These final comments also provided additional "glue" for the entire proceedings. The interrelationships of the papers so evident here is a virtue too often lacking in meetings of this sort.

I must admit a feeling of satisfaction about the symposium. The papers are of uniformly high quality and well written. The current thoughts of some of the best people in the field are represented. And significant and clear correspondences emerged. I am grateful to the participants for preparing so thoroughly.

The audiences for this book are psychologists and advanced undergraduate and graduate students interested in the areas of clinical, cognitive, motivation, and personality psychology. The book can serve as a main source of readings in courses on cognitive or motivational psychology and as a supplementary source for courses in clinical and personality psychology.

I am indebted to Cynthia Segersten for her aid in preparing the book and to the National Science Foundation, Grant GS-35216, for their support.

Cognition and Motivation:
Some Historical Trends

Robert C. Bolles

University of Washington

I am honored to have Professor Weiner invite me to participate in this conference, but also I feel somewhat uncomfortable about my role here. First, in the area of human motivation I am a little out of my element. The second reason for discomfort is that Weiner has asked me to provide some historical perspective on the problem of motivation and cognition, and this is a topic on which he himself has written the book (Weiner, 1972). Perhaps my best recourse in this situation is to seize the offensive by taking issue with Professor Weiner's book. One of the main themes of *Theories of Motivation* is indicated by its subtitle "From mechanism to cognition." Weiner maintains that the history of Psychology reveals a trend away from mechanism and toward a more cognitive approach to the explanation of behavior in general and the problems posed by human motivation in particular. His argument is supported at least in part by some of our history, but I will contend that it by no means tells the whole story. I will undertake to examine the history of this trend, embellishing Weiner's theme somewhat. Then I will move on to discuss briefly some other trends that I see in the history of motivation theory. Finally, I will risk some guesses as to how this field will be moving in the next few years. We will see that the other participants of the conference are moving with these trends, so that their work provides a remarkably contemporaneous and forward-looking view of the field. I will show how they have, wittingly or not, discerned the way things are moving and have moved on ahead, so that if we are to understand what is going to happen in motivation and cognition, they are the men we must follow. Theirs is the research we must understand.

In recent years there has indeed been a decline in the mechanistic philosophy and there has surely also been a resurgence of interest in cognitive

1

psychology. That much is true, but if we look back at earlier times we find that psychology did not begin from the mechanistic point of view. Quite the contrary, it is easy to make the case that psychology has always been more or less cognitive. Certainly it was initially so and it has continued to be so to a greater or lesser extent all along. Psychology's flirtation with the mechanistic philosophy was never much more than that. It may have looked as if the flirtation would become a real affair, and there were surely those who hoped to find a more permanent kind of relationship, but it was not to be — circumstances did not permit it. So psychology's yearnings to be united with the rest of science by becoming mechanistic was only an episode, a brief interlude. It was, fortunately, never more than that.

Probably the main attraction of the mechanistic philosophy was the belief that by espousing it we could more readily become scientists. But this was a misguided belief. In his marvelous short history of science, Singer (1959) made the point that science is not defined by or even characterized by its philosophical beliefs, but rather by its methods. The scientist is simply a man who places greater reliance upon data than upon dogma or *a priori* conviction; he is simply a systematic collector of data. Thus, a psychologist is a scientist by virtue of his systematic use of the empirical method and not because he studies behavior, or the brain, or because he abandons mentalistic phenomena, or turns away from cognitive processes. Thus, those psychologists who espoused a mechanistic philosophy were quite likely doing so for the wrong reasons, and their steadfast commitment to a mechanistic view of the world was, ironically, antithetical to the unbiased collection of data. But no one saw that. It took a man of Tolman's stature to make it clear. We will return to this point and particularly to Tolman's contribution to cognitive psychology a little later. First, though, let us look at our historical beginnings.

Plato was one of the early cognitive psychologists. He contended that, in general, men act so as to maximize the virtue attendant upon their acts. In effect, we all do what we perceive to be the right thing; we differ importantly, however, in what we preceive to be the right thing. For Plato, our ideas and our thoughts are based mostly upon cognitive processing. Our ideas reflected prior experience, to be sure, but they were not caused by prior experience. Plato was a nativist who believed that even our ideas are innately given. If we fail to apprehend a particular idea, it is not because we lack the idea but only that our perception of it is obscured. It is only through a proper education that our latent ideas (which are the ultimate causes of our behavior) can be clearly perceived. Man was assumed, of course, to be rational and to possess self-determination (later called free will), but our rationality and our will were governed in a gentle sort of way by our ideas or by our often distorted perception of our ideas. And in this Plato was a cognitive psychologist. He was not a thorough-going cognitive psychologist, though, because he was uncertain about either the rationality or the self-determination of women or animals. But for men, especially if they were Athenian freeholders, he left little doubt.

2

Although Plato did not distinguish sharply between the motivational and the non-motivational determinants of behavior, we may identify them for him. Rationality, the logical manipulation of ideas, is clearly an associative or structural factor. The will, or resolution, or determination, and the all-encompassing principle of seeking to maximize virtue are clearly motivational principles. The separation of structural and motivational factors became more explicit with St. Augustine and the other early Christian philosophers because they gave explicit attention to the factors determining the will. In the Christian era, Plato's optimistic virtue-seeking man became replaced with a less admirable theoretical person, a pleasure-seeking man.

For St. Augustine, man was literally torn asunder by the forces of pleasure and the forces of virtue. And it has taken us a good many centuries to begin putting together again what Augustine undid. But my point is that Augustine complicated Platonic man. Rather than one optimistic principle of motivation, there were two. Man could be motivated by good or by pleasure, and it was the predominance of one kind of motivation over another that justifies us judging our fellow man, blaming him if he is a pleasure-seeker or is otherwise base, and praising him if he seeks to serve others, or his god, or is otherwise noble. But what a man was, for St. Augustine, did not come entirely or even predominantly from his characteristic motives; it came from his thinking, from the kinds of perceptions and thoughts that he had. Like Plato, Augustine had a cognitive view of man in which at least the structural characteristics of personality were cognitive.

We can begin to see that for the early philosophers, the structural factors were the all important and yet complicated determinants of what a man is. Man was characterized primarily by the structural properties of his mind rather than by his motives. This was particularly true of the Christian philosophers, but it was also characteristic of Plato and other Greek philosophers as well. By contrast, the motivational principles of behavior were quite simple, unidimensional, almost monolithic in character; motives were merely either commended or condemned. The point I want to establish here is that because of the emphasis upon man's rationality as the basic explanation of his behavior, the original psychology of man in our culture was necessarily cognitive. I submit that that is the way it has always been, and that is the way the more conservative elements of our society still are. Our average man in the street, regardless of what he may have read of Freud or Skinner, still believes that he is rational, that his perceptions are unique, that his thoughts govern his acts, and that he is, as Socrates said, the measure of all things.

The history of our culture reveals, I think, another psychological assumption — the motivational determinants of what we are are relatively simple and relatively uninteresting. Consider how much has been written about how we perceive, how we come to know, how we remember, how we think and learn and work. Contrast the richness of this material with how little worthwhile has been written about our feelings, our emotions, and the kind of motives we have. The novelist, for example, in describing the characters of his story, will make them all different and we often see these differences as motivational. But consider how many pages it takes the novelist to convey, for example, that this person is loving and that that person is selfish. Consider how subtly and indirectly the message must be gotten across. We can recognize other men's motives in their behavior, but this perception of motives is subtle and we rarely talk explicitly about it. One reason appears to be that the English language is severely impoverished in this respect. Is it any wonder that in recent years new strange languages — the talk of the hippie and the talk of the person in group therapy — have had to be invented, and that these languages sound foreign to so many ears? Here for the first time a few people are beginning to communicate with some degree of efficiency about how they feel and about the reasons why they do the things they do. The shadow of St. Augustine still falls over us; we praise or (more often) blame a man because of his motives, but we are peculiarly inarticulate about personal motivations, even our own. The richness of our cognitive concepts and the poverty of our motivational concepts reflects a long historical tradition.

As we look back to the turn of the present century, we find that a cognitive view of man still prevailed; man was full of ideas and sensations. Man was cognitive in that he saw, and perceived, and thought. It was believed that if only we could understand how we perceive things, if only we could comprehend the structure of the mind, we would be on the way to explaining all psychological phenomena. By 1900, the conventional view of man, even the view of the conventional psychologists, was not only cognitive, it was also basically structural. The mind of man could be explained in terms of the structure of his ideas and perceptions, how these things were imbedded in the mind, and how they related to each other. It was to the explanation of these things that psychology was almost wholly dedicated. The cognitive and structural factors in psychology were emphasized at the expense of motivational factors. Even phenomena which were clearly motivational, such as emotion, were treated structurally. Emotions were dealt with by William James, for example, as structural elements. To understand an emotion, we must comprehend not what it does to us but rather we must seek to identify the stimulus that gives rise to the emotional feeling. This seems to have been the only aspect of emotion with which the early 20th century psychologists concerned themselves. Emotion was, in short, a structural characteristic and not a motivational factor. Psychology in 1900 was almost purely structural and almost purely cognitive.

But beginning about 1900 there came upon the scene a new and powerful idea which captivated many thoughtful and enterprising men. The idea was simply that the science of psychology could proceed faster by finding out how the brain works than by finding out anything about the structure of the mind. It was known from the work of the 19th century comparative physiologists that many responses of simple animals are merely reflexive reactions to stimulation. The behavior of the simplest animals could thus be explained in large part by simple S-R connections. It was easy enough to expand this elegant scheme, at least conceptually, to the complexities of human behavior. All behavior became, then, simply a matter of S-R connections. Some behaviors are, as with the simple animals, fixed by the genetic endowment. Other behaviors, for example, many of man's, are learned. The complex cognitive structure envisioned by the old fashioned psychologists was replaced with a new structure which, while still having a great deal of complexity for man, had the immense, irresistible virture of having a very simple syntax. It was no longer necessary to have all the old chapter headings: perceiving, thinking, remembering, feeling, reacting. There was just one kind of unit, the S-R connection. Instead of a whole host of cognitive processes, there was just the S-R Mechanism to explain all behavior. We may use the following simple diagram to illustrate the kind of explanatory system that the early behaviorists were advocating.

$$\underline{S} \rightarrow [S \text{-} R] \rightarrow \underline{R}$$

DIAG. 1. Conceptual System of Early Mechanistic Psychologists.
A stimulus, $\underline{S}$, stimulates a matrix of S-R units, which
generates a response, $\underline{R}$.

In a particular situation, there will be a physical event, usually the sensory reception of stimuli, which stimulates a matrix of S-R units, i.e., the S-R structure. Then this structure, all by itself, generates the response. The psychologists who advocated this simple scheme were also inclined to identify the theoretical S-R connection, the syntactical unit, with the empirical correlation that they found when they observed a response occurring in the experimental situation. That is, the S-R correlation became equated with a hypothetical neural S-R counterpart. Thorndike was perhaps the first psychologist to be guilty of this sin. He committed it in describing his cats in the puzzle box (Thorndike, 1898). Thorndike found that a learned response became gradually stronger and stronger in the puzzle box situation, and he assumed that this empirical correlation was produced by a corresponding brain process, an S-R connection, which gradually grew in strength in a corresponding manner. This may seem, in retrospect, like a strange assumption for Thorndike to have made, but consider what he gained by making it. First of all, it permitted him to be a behaviorist and to get systematic empirical data on the behavior of animals. He could do learning experiments and stimulate thousands of other psychologists to do more learning experiments. Second, by equating observable events with unobserved hypothetical processes, he solved in one stroke all of the philosophical issues that had developed around the mind-body problem. By attributing changes in the animal's behavior to hypothetical neural processes, he was applying the methods of science, or so he thought, to the problem of animal intelligence, which had hitherto not been a recognized part of science. Finally, he had an enormously simple theoretical system, at least from a syntactical point of view, because it only contained one kind of syntactical element, the S-R connection. The task of the psychologist interested in learning was simply to discover the structure of the S-R connections characteristic of a certain animal and see how they changed with experience.

It is interesting to note that in the original 1898 report of his animal experiments, Thorndike had no motivational principles at all. He tells us that the animal has to be hungry and has to obtain food upon exiting the puzzle box, but there were no motivational principles *per se* in his first theoretical framework. Such principles begin to emerge in Thorndike's 1911 account of the animal studies, and they become very prominent in his 1913 book on human psychology, *Educational Psychology*. Indeed, it could be said that the 1913 work was overlaid with such a plethora of motivational principles — concepts of belongingness, set, intention to learn, and so on — that Thorndike failed to convey a very coherent theoretical picture. In effect, he was too impressed with the richness and variety of human behaviors to be able to profit much from his own simple theory of learning.

Before leaving Thorndike altogether, it should be emphasized that he was not really a Mechanist.[1] He was tempted from time to time to speak about the neurons, how they are connected, and how their connections grew, but these statements should properly be regarded as peripheral to his psychological principles and not a fundamental part of either his philosophy of science or his psychological theorizing. I should hasten to add that Thorndike, while not a Mechanist, was not a cognitive psychologist either, because most of the vast array of phenomena that he studied and discussed were reduced theoretically to S-R mechanisms. One of my objections to Weiner's (1972) analysis of our history is that it leaves no place for a theorist like Thorndike (or for that matter,

---

[1] The word "mechanism" has unfortunately acquired a double meaning. On the one hand it means an explanatory regularity, a syntactical rule. The word is quite widely and quite properly used in this way. For example, the Freudian defense mechanisms are explanatory devices, hypothetical regularities which Freud invoked to explain otherwise inexplicable phenomena. It is important to recognize that for Freud the defensive mechanisms were cognitive in nature and in no sense mechanical in their operation. Mechanisms in the latter sense, i.e., to mean mechanical, will henceforth be spelled with a capital M to indicate that it means a doctrine, a philosophical position regarding the nature of the knowable reality. When it was first proposed, the S-R unit had the unfortunate circumstance of being both an explanatory mechanism, i.e., a syntactical or hypothetical rule, and also a Mechanism in the sense that it was a hypothetical physical entity, a tying together of neurons in the brain.

Hull) who shuns cognitive principles but also rejects the Mechanistic philosophy. Perhaps he is best classified simply as an S-R associationist.

One of the objections that his contemporaries raised regarding Thorndike was that he was too mentalistic. He was not scientific enough. He paid too little attention to the reality of the brain and its neural processes. This charge was made by John B. Watson, a man who we may characterize as both a mechanist and a Mechanist. Watson (1914) adhered to the program and the philosophy originally implied by Thorndike but which Thorndike himself apparently abandoned as soon as he started working with human subjects.[2] Watson adhered strictly to the scheme illustrated in Diagram 1. He had no motivational principles of any kind. Everything was reduced to structural terms. Even feelings were simple internal stimuli. All of the traditional contents of the mind, thoughts and such, were internal stimuli arising from the muscles. In effect, we don't really think; we only think we are thinking because we experience internal stimuli from the throat and elsewhere. Watson was perfectly willing to speculate about the location of these various internal stimuli even though there was in his time no possibility of monitoring them. We thus have the peculiar irony of a man proclaiming to be a super-scientist and throwing all of the tender-minded rascals out, but not being able to collect data to test the explanatory mechanisms that he was proposing. In spite of these terrible methodological problems, Watson's approach enjoyed enormous success; part of its popularity was because Watson was so effective a polemicist; part of it was because the traditional psychology, i.e., the 19th century mentalistic structuralism, had begun to collapse under its own weight; and part of Watson's success was because there was one element of very real virtue in his approach. By denying the mind and everything that had traditionally been associated with mentalism, and by emphasizing just the organism's behavior, it was possible to do systematic experiments and to find out a great deal about animals' behavior. Thus, Watson's methodological behaviorism proved to be a real achievement. His philosophical behaviorism, i.e., his Mechanistic philosophy, also continued to enjoy considerable success, but after just a few years it no longer continued to dominate psychological thought. Watsonian mechanisms prevailed, but his Mechanism was found wanting.

We should remember, however, that modern physiological psychologists often endorse a view similar to Watson's. Our contemporaries frequently emphasize the structural determinants of behavior and put these determinants into a theoretical mechanical system, like that illustrated in Diagram 2. Here we

---

[2] I refer to the change in theoretical style between Thorndike's 1898 and 1913 works. It is interesting that Freud too was originally a Mechanist but that when he went into practice with Breuer and had to cope with human behavior at a practical level he abandoned his Mechanistic philosophy, even though he still retained a rich variety of explanatory mechanisms whose historical origins had been mechanical (c.f., Bolles, 1975).

DIAG. 2. Conceptual System of Recent Physiological Psychologists. The behavioral effects of stimulation depends on a complex matrix of physiological factors.

see the structural matrix is much expanded to include not only S-R connections but also hormones, brain chemistry, various kinds of maturational effects, and prior experience effects. We are told that once all of these physical systems are understood and once we know how they develop over time, then all of psychology's questions will be answered. Whereas this ultimate hope does not appear to be very realistic at the present time, a variety of physiological approaches have revealed a dazzling array of interesting facts, and the whole enterprise has provided gainful employment for a number of people who can quite rightly call themselves psychologists. Perhaps time will ultimately prove them right, but I fear that their vindication will take a great deal of time, and in the meanwhile there is a lot of behavior to explain as best we can. At this point in our history, we must leave the Mechanists because their enterprise is quite different from what we are here to discuss. Let us just note that all during the 1920's a number of staunch defenders of the Mechanist philosophy sought to apply it uniformly to all of psychology. A number of writers contended that this was the only way really to explain behavior. But the Mechanistic era in psychology only lasted a few years. It dawned around 1900 and it gradually became replaced by other kinds of behavioristic systems in the 1930's. Perhaps the only true Mechanists were Watson and his immediate followers, and certain Russian reflexologists, most notably Bechterev (1913).

One further comment — if we look back at Diagrams 1 and 2, we can see that the matrix of structural events assumed to be necessary for the explanation of behavior has become considerably enlarged over the years. The scheme originally proposed by Thorndike and Watson (Diagram 1) was too simple. Diagram 2 still shows a single matrix, and it is still strictly structural, but it includes more different kinds of processes. The reason for this elaboration is simply that as we have found out more about behavior, we have found that it is somewhat more complicated than we originally proposed. As behaviorists continue to study in their own areas — the child psychologist working on developmental problems, the learning psychologist working on animal behavior, and so on — it has become necessary to hypothesize an ever-increasing network of explanatory mechanisms. If we look at the theoretical structure of a theorist like Hull (1943), who occupied a position intermediate in time, we find a situation like that shown in Diagram 3. Here we find two matrices. There is a new simple one containing the single monolithic motivational concept drive, D, and then there is a relatively elaborate but familiar matrix which includes the old S-R connection and some new factors such as inhibition and the oscillatory function, and other kinds of explanatory mechanisms. Two kinds of matrices to serve two kinds of explanatory purposes: one to explain motivation and one to explain the structure of behavior. This was an elegant, simple conceptualization. Altogether, the syntax of Hull's theory was considerably more elaborate than Watson's; it had to be elaborate to deal with all the new facts. The addition of the motivational matrix was deemed necessary by the discovery of animal motivation and the introduction of the structural complexities was made necessary by the discovery of other kinds of behaviorial phenomena. There were semantic complexities in Hull's theory too, but the most impressive change in behavior theory over the years has been the introduction of new explanatory devices and the necessary introduction of new syntactical rules telling us how to use these explanatory mechanisms to account for behavior.

$$\underline{S} \rightarrow \begin{bmatrix} {}_{S}{}^{H}{}_{R} \\ {}_{S}{}^{I}{}_{R} \\ \text{etc.} \end{bmatrix} \cdot [D] \rightarrow \underline{R}$$

DIAG. 3. Conceptual System of Hull's (1943) Theory.
Behavior depends upon the joint action of
motivational and structural matrices.

As we move closer to the present time, we find that the NeoHullians, such as Mowrer and Spence, have continued to add to the syntactical complexity of the basic explanatory model (see Diagram 4). Here we find a proliferation of motivational factors; accompanying drive there are incentive motivation, frustration, and acquired fear motivation. It is to the credit of the new Hullians, however, that they were ingenious enough to be able to simplify somewhat the structural matrix. The structural determinants of behavior were simpler for Spence than they were for Hull, even while the motivational determinants were more numerous and more complex. A further nicety of this kind of model from the point of view of learning theory was that the motivational matrix included learning mechanisms, i.e., classical conditioning, to augment the conventional learned S-R connection which was still an element of the structural matrix. The main point I wish to establish is that the discovery of new behaviorial phenomena in the animal laboratory necessitated the postulation of explanatory systems which were increasingly complex from a syntactical standpoint. More phenomena require further explanatory mechanisms. And let me point out again that this increase in syntactical complexity was at first most evident in the structural matrix and only in relatively recent times was the newer motivational matrix made more complicated.

$$\underline{S} \rightarrow \begin{bmatrix} {}_SH_R \end{bmatrix} \cdot \begin{bmatrix} D \\ r_G \quad r_F \\ Fear \end{bmatrix} \rightarrow \underline{R}$$

DIAG. 4. Conceptual System of Neo-Hullian Theorists, Including a Variety of Classically Conditioned Motivational Factors.

It could be argued that Skinnerian psychologists have reversed this trend. For the operant conditioner, the explanation of behavior lies in a very simple system in which the rate of a response is correlated with its contingent reinforcement. Typically, there is no motivation matrix, and the structural matrix consists of a simple kind of syntactical element, i.e., the reinforcement contingency. All this can be granted, but at the same time, it should be recognized that there are two considerations that seriously weaken the argument. One is that most theories of behavior aspire to generality; most theorists want to encompass all of the behavioral phenomena they can. Increased syntactical complexity is largely a result of an expanding perspective of the variety of behavior. By contrast, the Skinnerian has a scheme which is simple enough semantically, but just let him try to specify the boundary conditions within which it is effective! That's where the complexity resides. When will a given reinforcer on a given schedule be effective with a given organism so as to control a given response? The trouble here is that a reinforcement contingency is sometimes effective and sometimes not, and the *a priori* specification of the appropriate boundary conditions is an awesome task. The second consideration is that the Skinnerian methodology is designed to simplify the control of behavior rather than to reveal its natural inherent richness. Most of the interesting effects with human subjects show up in the first session or two. After the subject has pressed the button ten thousand times and collected his thousandth m & m, he may no longer be doing anything very interesting. Yet that is the point at which the Skinnerian typically starts looking at his cumulative records because that is where the behavior has stabilized.

We saw that by 1943 Hull had introduced into the mainstream of S-R associationism the conception of a simple motivating agency, D. The idea of motivation, of course, was not new with Hull. The idea of motivation apparently arose independently from several sources. McDougall stressed its importance as early as 1908. Freud had also seen its importance about the same time. But there was a peculiar reluctance on the part of mainstream psychologists to admit motivational principles. Pavlov had none. Watson surely had none. Thorndike had had a host of principles, but they were so diverse and so poorly articulated that he did not appear to be a motivation psychologist. But the phenomena of motivation were there; they only awaited systematic observation. It began with psychologists at Berlin, most notably Kurt Lewin, and, in this country, with Tolman. Tolman (1932) summarized a series of experiments done in his laboratory indicating that as the quality of the goal object was changed, or as the animal's need for the goal object was changed, there were predictable changes in an animal's behavior. Thus, Tolman introduced a matrix of new factors, which he called "demand" for the goal object, but which I will call *value*. The value matrix was assumed to contribute to behavior by acting upon, or motivating the use of, the structural determinants of behavior. Thus, it is largely to Tolman that we owe the introduction of the concept of motivation into animal psychology, from whence it made its way quickly into all of psychology. The concept probably would have gotten into human psychology, particularly the more applied areas, because of the work of Freud and others, but Tolman's unique contribution in this respect should be acknowledged.

Tolman made an even greater contribution. He saw quite clearly that the concept of habit as it has been developed by Thorndike and Watson and the advocates of classical conditioning was not really a behavioral concept. It had not arisen from the observation of behavior, at least not the behavior of intelligent organisms. The concept had been borrowed from the early physiologists working with very simple animal preparations. The S-R connection was, as we noted in discussing Thorndike, basically a physiological concept. It had a strong Mechanistic aura to it and hence did not properly describe the adaptive, intelligent, and apparently purposive behavior of the more intelligent animals, much less man. Tolman saw this and argued for this point of view as early as 1920. But at that time we were caught up in our romance with the Mechanistic philosophy and the force of Tolman's argument was lost for a number of years. Tolman contended that the concept of an S-R connection was a poor explanatory mechanism; it was too Mechanistic to explain behavior. Adaptive behavior requires for its explanation, he assumed, a mechanism with much more flexibility and looseness. Indeed, what we need to explain even the behavior of the rat in the maze is a set of syntactical rules, a mechanism, if you will, which has the free-wheeling properties of the conventional and traditional rational mind. We have to attribute to the animal, as well as to man, the ability to perceive relationships, the ability to remember one event and to anticipate another. The animal may have a belief that a particular event will be followed by another event, or a belief that a particular course of action will have certain consequences. The word which embodies these cognitive attributes is *expectancy*. Thus, for Tolman, behavior was the result of two types of matrices: a motivational matrix embodying constructs like the value of a goal object, and a second matrix which contained primarily the construct of expectancy (see Diagram 5).

11

$$\underline{S} \rightarrow [\text{Expectancy}] \ [\text{Value}] \rightarrow \underline{R}$$

DIAG. 5. Conceptual System Popularized by Tolman (1932).

Tolman's system was like Hull's (see Diagram 3) in that it took both motivational and the structural factors operating jointly to produce behavior. But this similarity was overshadowed by the important differences between Hull's and Tolman's positions. Hull was in the Mechanistic tradition; and although he was not really a Mechanist, as we have seen, he was in the Mechanistic tradition. Tolman was more in keeping with rationalistic tradition. His concept of expectancy defied the S-R connection and all the rest of the behavioristic machinery. Another major point of difference resided in the semantics of the two theories. For Hull, the analysis of any particular sample of behavior involved a great many semantic problems. What are the controlling stimuli? How often is a particular S-R connection reinforced? How much does inhibition generalize? Each of Hull's explanatory devices was fairly simple, but there was a host of them and their interrelationships provided the element of syntactical complexity that was necessary for the explanation of the complex phenomena that he studied. For Tolman, the structural matrix was smaller, it contained fewer elements; only various kinds of expectancy are found there. But an expectancy had very complex syntactical rules which introduced complexity into the syntax of Tolman's theory, which is precisely why Tolman proposed it. The attendant semantic problems arising from its application were simple but sophisticated. Once expectancy was given an operational definition it could be immediately applied to phenomena that were very difficult to explain from the Hullian point of view. The latent learning experiment is a case in point. Its explanation required a good deal of deviousness from the Hullian but was straightforward for Tolman. The place learning studies constitute another example where the Hullian was obliged, like Watson a generation before, to hypothesize the existence of unobserved controlling stimuli. Tolman's explanation was very simple: the rat expects food in a particular place, so it goes there when it is hungry. This, of course, is the great appealing virtue of a cognitive approach. Thus, the greatest debt we owe to Tolman is for introducing cognition back into psychology from whence it had been banished by Watson in his zeal to be scientific.[3]

---

[3] I wonder if it is merely accident that we are indebted to Tolman for introducing a cognitive orientation back into psychology and also for introducing motivation principles. Perhaps these contributions are inherently correlated. We may note that McDougall (1908) was both very cognitive and also very motivational. The same case could be made for Freud, i.e., that he too was a cognitive psychologist.

Tolman's expectancy times value model of behavior has constituted the basic framework for all subsequent cognitive models of behavior. It has provided the starting point for virtually all of us who claim to be cognitive psychologists. Let me just cite a couple of examples. Lewin (1936) proposed a motivational model of behavior that looks superficially different from Tolman's but it turns out to be not too different. It can be analyzed into a pair of matrices. One matrix consists of simple cognitive structural elements, namely, the means-end relationships perceived by the individual in a given situation. This is the so-called life space through which the organism must locomote, either literally or figuratively, by engaging in one kind of behavior as a means to another, or symbolically in terms of some kind of cognitive process which can alter the perception of the life space. The second matrix involves forces or tensions which make the individual seek particular goals. Lewin thus has a pair of matrices which can be put in correspondence with Tolman's, reading force toward the goal for value, and reading means-end relationship for expectancy. As Lewin himself noted, his model was an extremely simple one, really a pre-theory of behavior. It stated simply that if the organism perceives a way to get what he wants, he will do that.

Lewin's model was, of course, cognitive, but notice that, like Tolman's before it, the richness of syntax inherent in cognitive processes pertains primarily to the perception of means-end readinesses. This is where the subject must perceive and remember and where he can learn, and where he solves problems, symbolizes, and takes detours. In other words, the complexity of the total system is contained almost entirely in the structural matrix. The motivational matrix retains great simplicity. Again we are reminded of Hull's system (see Diagram 3) where the motivational matrix contained just a single term, D, which multiplied indiscriminately all the clear devices in the structural matrix. For Lewin, the motivational matrix was somewhat more complicated than this. Indeed, it had a number of syntactical properties of its own. An excess of tension in one motivational system could flow into other systems or even interact with the structural matrix and change the apparent boundaries of the life space. In other words, Lewin had begun to complicate the motivational matrix just as Spence and others were to complicate the originally simple Hullian motivational matrix. Of course, many of the phenomena which Lewin studied in his own laboratory were just these kinds of motivational effects.

The basic Tolman-Lewin model eventually became rather popular. It was adopted and elaborated by Rotter (1954) and applied to a variety of social learning situations. It was elaborated again by Atkinson (1964) and his colleagues and applied to the explanation of a variety of phenomena found in achievement motivation. It is interesting to note that Atkinson has further elaborated and complicated the motivational matrix so that instead of being a simple thing containing only the value of success, he recognizes two

13

factors – one a drive-like need for achievement and the second an incentive-type factor having to do with the value of success. There was a further elaboration of the motivation matrix by the introduction of fear of failure in addition to the hope of success. The parallels with the NeoHullian development of motivational theory should be apparent.

We may recap our history with these summary points. Originally, before psychology became an autonomous discipline, cognitive views of man prevailed. The early philosophers as well as the man of letters and the thoughtful layman all stressed man's rationality and explained his behavior in terms of ideas, perceptions and other intellectual activities. Then psychologists suffered that curious passion to be scientific. Thinking was merely a physical process going on in the brain; perception was merely the result of certain neural inputs; man was reduced to a mass of S-R connections; and behavior was explained by a vast matrix containing nothing but S-R units. This was an appealingly simple system but it was soon found to be inadequate even for the explanation of animal behavior. The revolt against this simplistic mechanical view was led by Tolman and others who found that there were motivational as well as structural determinants of behavior. The discovery of a variety of new phenomena led to the incorporation of more complex syntactical systems; this complexity appeared first in the structural factors and then in the newer motivational factors assumed to underly behavior. Those who retained the old S-R connection as an explanatory mechanism were obliged to supplement it with many other mechanisms. Meanwhile, there were those who contended that only cognitive processes had the inherent flexibility and richness necessary for the explanation of behavior. The number of syntactical elements could be reduced if the explanatory devices themselves were assumed to operate more flexibly.

In recent years, cognitive psychology has become increasingly popular and applied to an ever-widening variety of phenomena. Much of this new enthusiasm for cognitive explanatory models is attributable to the success of the information processing approach in such areas as human learning and memory. Cognitive psychology has been concerned with questions like what is the information-processing potential for the human subject, and how are different kinds of information assimilated, stored, and retrieved? It should be noted that much of the momentum that has carried the cognitive approach forward has been concerned with refining and elaborating the nature of the structural matrix. But the unique task which this conference has set for itself is the application of cognitive principles to motivational phenomena. Cognitive concepts are becoming applied not only to the structural determinants of behavior but to the motivational determinants as well. Indeed, motivation itself is becoming reconceptualized along cognitive lines. Let us see how some of the participants of this conference are moving in this direction.

14

One motivational phenomenon which has been almost ignored through most of the history of psychology is emotion and the role it plays in the determination of behavior. For years we were so convinced of the idea that an emotion was simply either a stimulus which gave rise to behavior, or was itself a response which produced stimuli which gave rise to behavior or motivation, that all of the interesting problems got shunted aside. But finally Lazarus has developed a very cognitive approach to emotion which gives a refreshingly new view of emotion, emotional expression, and how emotion affects behavior. Lazarus' analysis begins with the idea of "primary" appraisal: certain situations are perceived objectively as threatening or gratifying. Then this perception is said to give way promptly to a "secondary" appraisal in which the individual perceives himself in the situation. Among the implications of this perception is the importance of the individual's own ability, or inability, to cope with his emotion or with the threat posed by the situation.

In the paper he presents here, Lazarus describes a variety of different ways of coping with an emotion-invoking situation. Some techniques are natural in the sense that they involve innate behaviors, avoidance behaviors and the like — but other techniques involve individualized learned techniques for coping with threats, e.g., particular kinds of avoidance responses. He observes that many of our reactions to emotional situations are socially conditioned. We respond not only in terms of the situation but in terms of how we perceive we are supposed to react. One of the most interesting ways of coping with an emotional situation, however, is in terms of what Lazarus calls intrapsychic manipulation of the emotion itself. We may deny we are afraid. We may adopt an attitude of intellectual detachment from a situation that would otherwise frighten us. Thus, we see that there are a whole range of mechanisms which are, in effect, defense mechanisms against unpleasant emotions which permit the individual to deal with this important class of motivation variables. The proper study of emotion in man is therefore said to consist of an analysis of how an individual characteristically deals with different kinds of situations. This coping necessarily involves much of the cognitive capacity of the individual. We see, therefore, that the motivation matrix itself is not something set aside from the individual's cognitive processes but interacts directly with them. We see then that Lazarus' approach illustrates a trend not only toward conceiving of greater complexity in the motivation matrix, but of a wholly different order of complexity introduced by conceiving of the motivation matrix itself in cognitive terms. Cognitive principles, it seems, are becoming applied to both matrices and not just to the structural matrix, as was the case with Tolman and Lewin and the great majority of the intervening psychologists.

Lazarus' work illustrates a second trend. When S-R psychology was in its prime, particularly when it was in the hands of the Mechanists, man was regarded as a passive participant in his own psychological activities. We were all victims of our early learning experience. Even when the concept of the passive organism began to fade from view, there was still the tradition that we were victims of our own emotions. But Lazarus shows us that, quite the contrary, we deal actively with our own emotions, we cope with situations, we seek out situations in which particular emotional contents will occur, and then we deal with these in turn.

It should also be pointed out that Lazarus calls for a more naturalistic approach to the analysis of human behavior. Certainly much of his own research delves into real-life problems. One is struck by the parallels between this kind of inquiry and the dedication of the ethologists to study animal behavior in its natural setting. One also is struck by the artificiality of many of our favorite research paradigms. Without detracting from the importance of Pavlov's work, we must wonder how much Pavlov would have found out about learning had his dogs not been so constrained by the experimental situation (and Pavlov not been so constrained by his commitment to studying salivation) that no other behavior was recorded other than the number of drops of saliva produced. How much of our current thinking about the state of psychology is dictated by our habits of using memory drums or personality questionnaires or need-achievement type tasks? Someday we will know. But in the meanwhile it is refreshing to get a more naturalistic look at the kinds of problems with which psychologists concern themselves, whether they are dealing with human behavior or animal behavior.

I see one other trend here that I must comment upon, and that is that as learning and cognitive processes and other kinds of mechanisms become an intrinsic part of the motivational matrix, and to the extent that these are already a part of the structural matrix, we must wonder whether there is any justification for maintaining the distinction between the two kinds of matrices. We begin to suspect that a time will come when we can do with just one large matrix which will include both the motivational and structural determinants of behavior. Both kinds of determinants would be, of course, largely cognitive. Perhaps we are beginning to see that the distinction between the structural and motivational factors is an arbitrary one which arose naturally enough because of the peculiar heritage forced upon us by S-R associationism. That is, once we had the S-R mechanism to explain behavior, it became necessary to introduce a new class of behavioral determinants when motivational phenomena were discovered. But when we are free of the S-R heritage and can become comfortable with a cognitive model, i.e., with models whose basic syntactical properties are complex enough to deal with the richness of human behavior, we will no longer feel a necessity to make a distinction between structure and the motivation of the structure.

I see Mischel's paper on emotion as similar to Lazarus' in several respects. He advocates an interactionist position whereby a particular motivational state,

16

frustration, can be dealt with by the human subject in different ways with different implications for behavior. An important aspect of Mischel's investigations is that he is working with youngsters who have not yet learned to use their cognitive processes to deal effectively with the emotional state resulting from deferred reward. Even so, they have ways of assimilating events over long reaches of time. And he finds a clear interaction between the kinds of cognitive processes which have always been assumed to be a part of the structural matrix and the motivational matrix (an emotion in this case) which has conventionally been viewed as being relatively independent of cognitive intervention. His work also illustrates the trend toward thinking of an active (rather than a passive) organism. And, of course, Mischel is deeply concerned with what may be a uniquely human attribute, namely, the ability to delay gratification. The study of this attribute lends an air of naturalism and natural interest to his work.

The recent work of Atkinson and his collaborators at Michigan provides further illustration of some of these new points of view. Atkinson and Birch (1970) tell us it is artificial to think of motivation as a special kind of causal event. It is not the case that there are motivated behaviors and unmotivated behaviors. Nor is it the case that behavior arises when there is some appropriate motive for it. Such ideas reflect, again, the old-fashioned belief in the passivity of the individual. The fact of the matter is that all of the people and all of the animals we know are always busy doing something. The explanation of their behavior, we are told, lies not so much in searching out the motives for what they are doing at a particular time but in explaining why they persist in doing what they are doing, and why, after having persisted so long, they quit and begin doing something else. Behavior is a stream, a continuity of acts. In the present paper, Birch, Atkinson, and Bongart tell us that the changes in behavior reflect temporal changes in cognitive processes. So again we can have the concept of one big cognitive matrix. The concept of motivation becomes largely superfluous, as I understand the Birch, Atkinson, and Bongart position. That is to say, there are not structural and motivational determinants of behavior; there is simply the ongoing stream of behavior and the task of the psychologist is to find out what modulates the stream. Birch, Atkinson, and Bongart's own guesses as to the modulation factors are that they are very cognitive. More specifically, as the individual thinks about this and that, these thoughts may instigate appropriate kinds of behavior or lead to the abandonment of others.

I think that this view of behavior is inevitably going to lead to much freer and more unstructured observation of peoples' activities. Rather than requiring our subjects to perform trial after trial on some learning task, or to fill in one item after another on a questionnaire, and building a theory around the data obtained from such highly structured observations, we will spend a lot of time simply looking at the behavior of people in their natural settings. We are also going to have to develop new techniques simply to describe naturally occurring behavior (e.g., Seltzer & Sawusch, 1974). But when we begin to watch human behavior in more natural circumstances, we will discover that they have some curious and uniquely human attributes, one of which, as we noted earlier, is that humans can delay gratification and can weld together events that occupy vast reaches of time. At least under certain circumstances they can. With this idea in mind, Raynor (1974) has attacked the artificiality of the conventional need-achievement experiment. Raynor has observed that what is called success within the context of the experiment may simply be an instrumentality of the individual for achieving some further goal through the establishment of his own self-image as a successful achiever. This goal may in turn be an instrumentality for success in school, which may in turn be instrumental in his lifetime goals, and so on. Raynor has found a variety of elegant predictions from a new breed of achievement studies in which subjects reveal not only their need to succeed in a particular arbitrary task, but also something about their whole life styles.

One of the ways in which the dichotomy between structure and motivation has gradually and quietly broken down over the years is with the discovery of what are sometimes called cognitive needs. In recent years, a great deal of work has gone into demonstrating in one way or another that cognitive processes do interact with an individual's motivation. Rotter (1954) had given us the basic distinction between internal and external reference. A number of psychologists have gone on from there to develop the concept that some people are dependent upon themselves, whereas others are dependent upon others. It remained only for Fritz Heider (1958) to call attention to the fact that an important aspect of an individual's cognitive makeup is how and to what he attributes the causation of the things that happen to him. Weiner develops this topic here briefly and in much more satisfying detail in his book (Weiner, 1972). The basic idea is that in performing a particular task a given individual may attribute his success or failure, as the case may be, to either internal events (his own ability or his own effort) or to external events (the difficulty of the task or luck). Weiner has discovered that high and low need achievers differ not only in their motivation for success and the incentive value that success at the task holds for them, they differ just as importantly, and perhaps more basically, in the causes to which they attribute their success and failure. For example, a high need-achiever is typically willing to take all the credit for his own success. This attribution system maintains the high need-achiever's self regard. This concept of characteristic ways of attributing causation to events in the world around us is perhaps as basic to an understanding of social-psychological phenomena and personality dynamics as it is in the understanding of more conventional human learning and motivation situations.

The existence of such phenomena illustrates again the same trends we have just noted. There is a trend away from passivity; the subject does not just process information about the outcomes of his behaviors, he makes something of this information. He pigeon-holes and characterizes it, and makes what is for him, cognitive sense of it. At the same time he characterizes and makes sense out of himself and the world around him. We can see that while the substance of these motivational propositions are cognitive, the effects of a particular kind of attribution can, in turn, affect the individual's motivation. For example, how we handle causal attribution determines, at least in part, not only what we expect from our acts but also how we will value the outcome. Aesop's fox who could not reach the grapes did not reach the realistic conclusion that he was incapable of doing so, but the distorted conclusion that the grapes weren't worth having (the fox was evidently a high need-achiever). Cognitive dissonance research has provided a mass of illustrations in the last few years of the principle that maintaining the integrity of one's causal attribution system can lead to gross distortions of other cognitive processing. So again we see quite clearly an interaction between the motivational determinants and the cognitive processes that have traditionally been viewed as structural determinants of the individual's behavior.

$$\left[\begin{array}{c} \text{Cognitive} \\ \text{Processes} \end{array} \right] \rightarrow \underline{R}$$

DIAG. 6. Conceptual System for Current Cognitive Motivational Models. Note that input to the system is not necessary, and that a separate motivational matrix is not needed.

The trend is clearly toward a single big matrix rather than two smaller ones (see Diagram 6). Diagram 6 lacks, we may note, an input arrow on the stimulus side. This is not to say that we do not respond to stimulation, but its absence emphasizes the point that we are not dependent upon stimulation; we are not passive. Cognitive processes in and of themselves generate plenty of behavior. And, of course, Diagram 6 illustrates that there may be a multitude of new kinds of cognitive mechanisms involved in the determination of behavior. I predict that there is going to be a rich diversity of hypothesized cognitive mechanisms.

I predict, too, that if anyone ever achieves theoretical closure and gives us a satisfactory, small set of cognitive mechanisms that have claim to broad generality for the human subject, he will be a very astute and perceptive theorist indeed. I will also predict that when this theorist arrives upon the scene, he will provide us with a system which contains just one matrix containing both motivational and structural mechanisms; I predict that both kinds of mechanisms will be cognitive; that he will assume man to be active rather than passive; and that he will support his theoretical position by systematically observing what people do in naturalistic settings.

But enough of historical observations and prognostications. Let us move on to see where we stand at the moment.

REFERENCES

Atkinson, J.W. *An introduction to motivation*. Princeton: Van Nostrand, 1964.

Atkinson, J.W., and Birch, D. *Dynamics of action*. New York: Wiley, 1970.

Bechterev, V.M. *La psychologie objective*. Paris: Alcan, 1913.

Bolles, R.C. *Theory of motivation*, 2nd ed. New York: Harper and Row, 1975.

Heider, F. *The psychology of interpersonal relations*. New York: Wiley, 1958.

Hull, C.L. *Principles of behavior*. New York: Appleton-Century-Crofts, 1943.

Lewin, K. *Principles of topological psychology*. New York: McGraw-Hill, 1936.

McDougall, W. *An introduction to social psychology*. Boston: Luce, 1908.

Raynor, J. Future orientation: The cognitive elaboration of a theory of achievement motivation. In J.W. Atkinson and J.O. Raynor (Eds.), *Motivation and achievement*. Washington: V.W. Winston, 1974.

Rotter, J.B. *Social learning and clinical psychology*. Englewood Cliffs: Prentice-Hall, 1954.

Seltzer, R.C., and Sawusch, J.R. A program for computer simulation of the dynamics of action. In J.W. Atkinson and J.O. Raynor (Eds.), *Motivation and achievement*. Washington: V.W. Winston, 1974.

Singer, C. *A short history of scientific ideas to 1900*. Oxford: Oxford University Press, 1959.

Thorndike, E.L. Animal intelligence: An experimental study of the associative processes in animals. *Psychological Review Monograph Supplement*, 1898, *2*, No. 8.

Thorndike, E.L. *Animal intelligence*. New York: Macmillan, 1911.

Thorndike, E.L. *Educational psychology*. New York: Teachers College, 1913.

Tolman, E.C. Instinct and purpose. *Psychological Review*, 1920, *27*, 218-233.

Tolman, E.C. *Purposive behavior in animals and man*. New York: Appleton, 1932.

Watson, J.B. *Behavior: An introduction to comparative psychology*. New York: Holt, 1914.

Weiner, B. *Theories of motivation*. Chicago: Markham, 1972.

Cognitive and Coping Processes in Emotion

Richard S. Lazarus

University of California, Berkeley

Although the title of this symposium refers only to motivation, many of the same issues about the role of cognition are also found in the closely related problem of emotion. I believe that emotion too cannot be understood or even adequately researched without asking about the cognitive factors underlying the emotional reaction. It has always seemed to me that when Freud (1936) spoke of anxiety in his monograph *Inhibitions, Symptoms, and Anxiety* as arising from the perception of danger, he was pointing the way toward a cognitive approach to emotion. The unanswered implicit question he posed there concerns the rules by which danger is recognized or cognized by the person or the ego-system.

My presentation here has two main themes: First, that cognitive processes determine the quality and intensity of an emotional reaction; and second, that such processes also underlie coping activities which, in turn, continually shape the emotional reaction by altering the ongoing relationship between the person and the environment in various ways. Let me begin with the first theme.

From my point of view (Lazarus, Averill, & Opton, 1970), emotions reflect the continuing nature of the person's or animal's adaptive commerce with his environment and the way this commerce is evaluated. The commerce can be judged by him as either damaging, threatening, challenging, or conducive to positive well-being. Each of us maintains special motives, belief systems, and competencies to cope with problems, and each also arranges and interprets his commerce with the environment in particular ways. *Cognitive appraisal* is the cornerstone of my analysis of emotions; and this appraisal, from which the various emotions flow, is determined by the interplay of personality and the environmental stimulus configuration.

From this perspective, emotion is defined in the following way: It is a complex disturbance which includes three main components — namely, subjective affect (which includes the cognitive appraisal), physiological changes related to species-specific forms of mobilization for action, and actions having both instrumental and expressive features. The somatic disturbance arises from an impulse to action which, in part, defines the particular emotion and reflects the mobilization for the action. The quality or intensity of the emotion and its action impulse depend on a cognitive appraisal of the present or anticipated significance of the adaptive commerce for the person's or animal's well-being. In lower animals, such as those studied by Tinbergen, the evaluative or appraisal feature of the emotion-eliciting perception is built into the nervous system. In higher mammals, such as man, symbolic thought processes and learning play a predominant role.

In stressing the importance of cognitive appraisal in the mediation of emotional states, it is useful to point to a debate between Hans Selye, with his "general adaptation syndrome" (GAS) on the one hand, and John Mason and I on the other. Selye argues that the GAS is a universal biological defense reaction aroused by any physically noxious agent. Mason (1971) points out, however, that coping processes are constantly shaping the endocrine response to stressor conditions. To express this mediation of the physiological response by coping and other psychological processes, Mason used the compound term "psychoendocrinology," thus attributing to psychological processes an important portion of the variance in endocrine reactions under noxious conditions. Mason and I have gone even further in this direction: We both have suggested (Lazarus, 1966; Mason, 1971) that the essential mediator of the GAS may be *psychological*. Therefore, we are saying that the pituitary-adrenal cortical response to disturbed commerce with the environment may require that the animal or person somehow recognize his plight. Any animal that has sustained an injury is apt to sense that he is in trouble; and if he does not, there will be no GAS. Moreover, in research on the GAS, psychological mediation has almost never been ruled out. Thus, one could argue with some justification that this cognitive appraisal of harm via cerebrally controlled processes is necessary to initiate the body's defensive adrenal cortical response.

An animal that is unconscious can sustain bodily harm without the psychoendocrine mechanisms of the "general adaptation syndrome" becoming active. Data from Symington et al. (1955), for example, suggest that unconsciousness and anesthesia eliminate the adrenal effects of physiological stress. In their study, patients who were dying from injury or disease showed a normal adrenal cortical condition as assessed during autopsy as long as they have remained unconscious during the period of the fatal condition. In contrast, patients who were conscious during the periods of the fatal disease process did show adrenal cortical changes. A study by Gray et al. (1956) has also demonstrated that general anesthesia, by itself, does not produce a significant adrenal reaction. These studies raise the question of whether it is the *psychological significance of injury* rather than its physiologically noxious effects that produce the adrenal cortical changes associated with stress.

We have a great need for a transactional language that describes individual differences in the way a person relates to the environment. I have constructed a simple hypothetical example to bring the point home. Consider two different persons who perceive that they are facing a demand, or the juxtaposition of several demands, which seem to them to be at the borderline or beyond their capacity to master — too much is expected of them. As a result of their individual histories and particular personalities, Person A feels that failure of mastery reflects his own inadequacy, while Person B, by contrast, feels the same pressure but interprets the situation as one in which people are constantly trying to use or abuse him. Both experience similar degrees of anticipatory stress and are mobilized to cope with the problem. Prior to the confrontation with the dangerous situation, both experience anxiety, an anticipatory emotion produced by appraised threat. In Person A, the anxiety is mixed with depression, while in Person B, the anxiety is mixed with external blaming and anger. Following the confrontation in which both perform badly, Person A will experience mainly loss and depression, while Person B mainly anger and resentment. Thus, a similar set of overwhelming demands has been construed or appraised quite differently by these two individuals. If, on the other hand, these persons do well in the confrontation, one may experience more elation than the other, depending on whether the explanation of the success is luck or their own perseverance and skill. In any case, such subtle differences in appraisal of a stressful commerce with the environment underlie variations among individuals in the severity (and possibly the pattern) of bodily reactions, the intensity and chronicity of the accompanying emotion, the quality of the affects experienced, and the types of solutions for which they opt, including seeking and accepting clinical help.

You will recognize that in this analysis of cognitive appraisal and emotion I come close to the efforts of attribution theorists, such as Bernard Weiner in this symposium, to spell out the cognitions underlying variations in achievement striving and the person's response to success and failure. Such concepts, in my view, can defeat circularity by leading to the identification of variables within the person and in the situation producing particular kinds of cognitive mediations and one or another type of action.

There is, incidentally, a tendency, especially in psychological research on emotion in the laboratory, to focus only on the immediate stimulus situation that provokes an emotion, while forgetting what is or has been going on in the general life of the person, as if the latter did not exist and played no role. An emotion then becomes an immediate "figure" in the person's life, so to speak, with the "ground" simply ignored. The person is momentarily occupied by certain transactions with the environment (his or her figure), but there remains a background of other problems, concerns, moods, and emotions that might well be considered in our attempts to understand emotions in nature. Perhaps the person has been struggling with multiple problems about which he may feel

23

despair or depression much of the time, and suppressing such feelings as much as possible. He goes to work (or into our laboratories) and fulfills the day to day demands of his responsibilities against this depressive background. Although we know almost nothing about the possible interpenetrations of the figure and the ground of emotion, there may be important dynamic relationships. For example, the ongoing activities of the job (the figure) may suddenly make salient the wider problems being faced outside of the work situation in such a way as to elicit anger or depression then and there. Or, perhaps the job activities are sought out as ways of mastering, or at least momentarily preventing through attention deployment, a general sense of despair. In short, whatever the person is momentarily experiencing, be it emotional or not, happens against a background of other psychological conflicts and states, even if these are tentatively pushed into the background. This background of latent emotionality is constantly lurking in the shadows and is undoubtedly a major influence on the immediate figure states, just as is the immediate stimulus.

Now what about the second theme concerning coping or self-regulation? Emotion is not a constant thing. Rather, it ebbs and flows and changes over time as the nature of the adaptive commerce and the information about it changes. Anger suddenly melts and changes to guilt, depression, relief, or love; anxiety changes to relief or euphoria; guilt changes to anger; and so on. Most strong emotional states are complex and have more than one quality; emotions typically involve complex combinations of affect, each deriving from multiple cognitive appraisal elements to be found in any complex human transaction with the environment. These shifts in intensity and quality over time reflect perceived and evaluated or appraised alterations in the person's relationship with the environment, based in part on feedback from the situation and from his own reactions. In the stress emotions, the changes reflect, in part, the person's constant efforts to master the interchange by overcoming the damage, by postponing or preventing the danger, or by tolerating it. Thus, as a result of constant feedback and continuing efforts to cope with the situation or to regulate the emotional response, the person is also constantly reappraising his relationship with the environment, with consequent alterations in the intensity and quality of the emotional reaction. Thus, expectations about his power to deal with the environment and master danger are a factor in determining whether the person will feel threatened or challenged by what happens.

This latter theme is especially important for an understanding of emotional states because it places emphasis not only on cognitive processes, but also on *coping processes* as central features. We are sometimes accidentally confronted by a situation having major relevance for our welfare, but we also do a great deal of active regulating of our emotional reactions. People select the environments to which they must respond; they shape their commerce with it, plan, choose, avoid, tolerate, postpone, escape, demolish, manipulate their attention, and also deceive themselves about what is happening, as much as possible casting the relationship in ways that fit their needs and premises about themselves in the world. In regulating their emotional life, they are also thereby regulating the bodily reactions which are an integral part of any emotional state.

There are countless observations of the important role played by such coping activities in emotion. In a previous discussion of these (Lazarus, 1973), I cited everyday life anecdotal examples, such as the management of grief, the escalation or discouragement of a love relationship, and being a good loser. I also cited formal research examples, such as field studies of combat stress, the psychoendocrine research of the Bethesda group on parents of children dying of leukemia (Wolff et al., 1964), the observations of Lief and Fox (1963) on reactions to viewing a medical autopsy, and research from my own laboratory (Koriat, et al. 1972) dealing with the self-control of emotional states. There is insufficient time here to do full justice to the problem, but it will be useful to illustrate two interesting examples of the role of intrapsychic as opposed to direct-action coping processes.

Lief and Fox (1963) have conducted extensive interviews with medical students witnessing a medical autopsy for the first time — an experience that can be quite distressing. Students, who are probably self-selected to a high degree, usually achieve detachment from the experience, though there are some failures to do so, too. Certain institutional features of the procedure itself provide help to the student in the process of achieving detachment. For example, during the autopsy the room is immaculate and brightly lit and the task is approached with seriousness and a professional air which helps achieve a clinical and impersonal attitude toward death. Certain parts of the body are kept covered, particularly the face and genitalia. The hands, which are so strongly connected with human, personal qualities, are usually not dissected. Once the vital organs are removed, the body is taken from the room, bringing the autopsy down to mere tissues which are more easily depersonalized. The deft touch, skill, and professional attitudes of the prosector make the procedures neater and more bloodless than might otherwise be the case, and this increases intellectual interest and makes it possible to approach the whole thing scientifically rather than emotionally. Students avoid talking about the autopsy; and when they do, the discussion is impersonal and stylized. Finally, humor, which is typical as a defense in laboratory dissection, is absent in the autopsy room, perhaps because joking would appear too insensitive in the case of recent death. In short, the student struggles to achieve a proper balance between feeling things and looking at them objectively, an effort in which detachment or distancing is facilitated by a variety of institutional procedures. Some professional individuals in medicine and nursing appear to overdo the coping strategy of detachment and are seen by their patients as cold and indifferent.

The second example is, I believe, the only experimental psychophysiological study explicitly designed to investigate whether and how people can alter their emotional states volitionally. Arguing that most research in the area of emotional control has been oriented to the *reduction* of stress reactions, while healthy management of one's emotional life requires also the *release* of emotional reactions, as in love, empathy, joy, distress over the suffering of others, etc., my colleagues and I (Koriat et al., 1972) instructed laboratory subjects to do both. In two experimental sessions they were exposed to four presentations of a film showing wood-shop accidents in which one man lacerates the tips of his fingers, another cuts off his middle finger, and a third dies after a plank of wood is thrust through his midsection by a circular saw. During the first two presentations there were no special instructions. However, half the subjects were instructed prior to the third presentation to *detach* themselves from the emotional impact of the accidents, and before the fourth presentation they were asked to *involve* themselves more fully and emotionally in them. The other half were given reverse order instructions, that is, on the third film presentation they had to involve themselves, while on the fourth, to detach themselves. They were not told how to do this, since one of the objectives of the experiment was to evaluate the cognitive devices they might use.

Among the findings of the research, two are of particular interest here. First, it was found that subjects could indeed exercise some degree of control over their emotional reactions to the accidents, as evidenced by their reported emotional state and changes in heart rate. Second, certain strategies were reported being used most commonly in involvement, and others in detachment. The most frequently reported *involvement* device was trying to imagine that the accidents were happening to the subject himself. Other less frequent strategies included trying to relate the scene to a similar experience he had or to which he was a witness, and trying to think about and exaggerate the consequences. The most popularly reported *detachment* strategy was reminding oneself that the events were dramatized for the film rather than being real, followed by the strategy of concentrating on the technical aspects of the production. In this study, we see clearly the operation of self-generated rather than situationally-induced modes of emotional control.

I have thus far avoided making explicit some of the theoretical issues or controversies inherent in this way of viewing emotion and its self-regulation by means of intrapsychic (cognitive) mechanisms, and some of these should now be examined.

(1) WHAT IS BEING REGULATED?

In speaking of the self-regulation of emotion, I have actually meant control not only over the overt behavior that can be associated with an emotion (e.g., the expressive gestures and postures and instrumental action), but of the entire organized state that is subsumed under the emotion construct.

There would be little argument that we are capable of inhibiting emotional behaviors such as avoidance, aggression, etc., or the behavioral expression of emotions such as grief, love, depression, and joy. I am saying, of course, more than this, namely, that intrapsychic forms of coping such as detachment, denial, etc., are also capable of modifying, eliminating, or changing the emotion itself, including its subjective affect and the bodily states which are a normal feature of it. When successful, these mechanisms not only modify the outward signs of emotion, but they dampen or eliminate the entire emotional syndrome. Thus, in the Bethesda studies of parents with children dying of leukemia (Wolff et al., 1964), by denying the fatal significance of their child's illness the Bethesda parents were no longer as threatened, and they exhibited lower levels of adrenal cortical stress hormones, than those parents who acknowledged the tragic implications; and by successfully distancing themselves from the personal emotional features of the autopsy, the medical students observed by Lief and Fox not only behaved unemotionally, but in all likelihood, if the appropriate measurements had been made, reacted with little or no affect and without the bodily disturbances that are an integral part of any stress emotion.

Moreover, much coping activity is anticipatory; that is, the person anticipates a future harmful confrontation such as failing an examination, performing in public, or confronting a flood, tornado, or a personal criticism, and such anticipation leads him to prepare against the future possibility of harm. To the extent that he prepares effectively, overcoming or avoiding the danger before it materializes, or being better able to function adequately in the anticipated confrontation, he thereby changes the nature of the ultimate transaction, along with the emotions that might have been experienced in the absence of such anticipatory coping. Overcoming the danger before it materializes can lead to exhilaration rather than fear, grief, depression, or whatever, depending upon the nature of the harm or loss that might have been experienced and the appraisal of the reasons for success.

You will note that this analysis reverses the usual wisdom that coping always follows emotion (or is caused by it) and suggests that coping can precede emotion and influence its form or intensity. In fact, my general position requires the assertion that coping never follows emotion in anything but a temporal sense, a stance in direct opposition to the longstanding and traditional view that emotions (such as anxiety) serve as drives or motives for adaptive behavior. The exception to this is when the person is trying to regulate the bodily state directly, but more about this in a moment.

Unfortunately, the psychology of coping is largely descriptive in nature, rather than systematic and predictive. People use a wide variety of coping processes, depending on their personal characteristics, the nature of the environmental demands and contingencies, and how these are appraised. They engage in a variety of preparatory activities. For example, they may worry without taking adequate steps to increase their effectiveness in confrontation, they reduce intense arousal by periodic disengagements from stressful transactions; they take tranquilizers to lower excessive levels of arousal; they use antispasmodics to quiet their bowels; they practice positive mental attitudes; they try to tell themselves that the problem will work itself out or that there is really no problem; they seek support from loved ones or those they trust; they try this or that stress-prevention fad or fashion, such as transcendental meditation, psychotherapy, relaxation, hypnosis, yoga, etc.; they direct their attention away from the source of threat and toward benign or escapist literature or movies; they cope with loss ultimately by giving up what was previously a central portion of their psychological domain. However, we still know extremely little about the conditions, both within the person and in the stimulus configuration, that lead to one or another coping process. We also know little about the relative effectiveness of such diverse coping processes in regulating emotional states or about the comparative costs in energy and other maladaptive consequences of each form of coping.

(2) WHAT IS THE MODE OF SELF-REGULATION?

Here I should make a distinction of importance between two kinds of emotion-regulatory processes – a distinction others too have made (cf. Mechanic, 1962). One type, which might properly be called "coping," concerns efforts by the person to deal with the problem generating the stress emotion in the first place. Whether the person takes direct action, say by attacking or escaping the harmful agency, or engages in intrapsychic forms of coping (which we typically refer to as defense mechanisms), the focus of the coping effort is on the plight in which the person finds himself. The other type, which might be called "direct control" of emotion, is focused on ways of reducing the visceral or motor reactions that are part of the stress emotion generated by troubled commerce with the environment.

For example, if a student who is facing an important and very threatening examination spends the anticipatory interval reading relevant books and articles, rehearsing his understanding of the subject matter with other students or teachers, trying to guess or find out the questions that will be asked, and so on, he is engaged in coping with the problem whether he does this effectively or ineffectively. He is attempting to alter his basic relationship with the environment or, put differently, to change the nature of his troubled commerce with it. To the extent that such activity leads to a more benign appraisal of the potential outcome of the examination – for example, by giving him a sense of preparedness and mastery – the emotional reaction attendant on the threatening character of the situation for him is to some extent short-circuited. His anxiety is reduced, along with its bodily concomitants, and he is better able to sleep, think, draw upon his knowledge in the examination, etc. From the standpoint of the emotional state, it does not matter whether or not he has been kidding himself about his mastery, although, of course, it will ultimately matter during or after the exam, say if he fails.

On the other hand, if the same student takes tranquilizers or drinks to control his disturbed bodily state, takes sleeping pills, engages in muscle relaxation, diverts his attention for a time, or tries other techniques designed to quiet his heightened arousal, he is seeking directly to control the emotional response itself rather than to cope with the environmental transaction which generated the arousal in the first place. He is dealing with the somatic reaction rather than its cause. In all likelihood the rules by which these two divergent kinds of processes operate are quite different.

I do not intend any derogation of this latter, response-oriented or peripheral approach. We all use a variety of emotion-regulating devices, including those involving direct-control activities, and this often helps greatly. Sometimes they are the only ones available to the person, perhaps because the tendency to appraise certain situations as threatening is very deep-rooted, or the source of threat is unknown and therefore fairly refractory to change. Moreover, as in the handling of test anxiety, sometimes effective coping in the problem-oriented sense is severely impaired by the emotion itself, as when the person finds he cannot think clearly about his problem and prepare adequately in the face of the interfering effects. Under such conditions, reducing the anxiety or the correlates of anxiety by *any* means available may serve to facilitate adaptive coping.

Moreover, in chronic or repeated situations of threat, even merely lowering debilitating arousal may swing the balance of the approach-avoidance conflict in favor of approach and commitment and away from avoidance and disengagement, and this may make possible the attainment of goals of great importance. For example, I am usually very uneasy about commercial flying, although I have flown extensively for much of my professional life. Were I not able to subdue my apprehensions and calm my overactive viscera on landings and takeoffs by alcohol or meprobamate, I might eschew making trips to professional meetings, with the attendant loss of important professional commitments and ultimate damage to my life goals. You will recognize, incidentally, that emotional control which aims at direct management of somatic turmoil rather than at the resolution of its psychodynamic origins is the arena in which biofeedback research and its use in therapy falls. We need to have more knowledge of the myriad forms of self-regulation that are available and serviceable to given kinds of people and in given types of situations in managing their emotional lives.

(3) WHY SELF-REGULATION?

In speaking of the control of emotion by means of intrapsychic processes, I have deliberately used the expression "self-regulation" to convey the theme that it is the person, appraising the personal and social requirements of an emotional situation, who manages his emotional reactions willfully, as it were, rather than merely passively and automatically responding to internal and environmental pressures.

The concept of self-regulation (often called self-control and sometimes impulse-control) has a long history, especially in clinical and personality psychology. It is also a common-sense or lay concept. To some, self-regulation might suggest a flirtation with the philosophical idea of free will or a quarrel with determinism. Yet the concept does not require that such acts of will or self-control be said to occur outside of natural laws, or that we cannot discover the determinants of self-control, some of which lie within the person.

When behaviorally-oriented psychologists have spoken of self-control, they have done so in what I consider to be a strange and contradictory way. Skinner (1953), for example, speaks of it as manipulating one's own behavior just as one might do in the case of another person or, as the environment does, through its pattern of reward and punishment contingencies. To decrease an undesirable behavior in oneself, for instance, the person makes the undesirable response less probable by altering the variables of reward and punishment on which it depends. Thus, if a person wishes not to overeat, he can place a time-lock device on the door of the refrigerator to eliminate snacks between meals. To prevent shopping sprees, he can leave his credit card or money at home. Thus, in this view, which has become exceedingly popular in behavior modification circles, the key agency of control seems to be the environmental contingencies rather than the person.

Although such environmental contingencies are very important, what is often missed is that an *executive agency within the person* determines which of many competing trends and impulses are to be encouraged or discouraged. Oftentimes it is not the environment that is manipulated, but what the person attends to in that environment, or how he interprets that environment. This is precisely what is meant by intrapsychic or cognitive control mechanisms. To speak of manipulating environment contingencies seems contradictory to me because it makes the environment the locus of self-control rather than the person, and this emphasis distorts the meaning inherent in the term *self*-control. It is the person who makes a commitment or decision on the basis of cognitive activity, whether he is conscious of it or not.

While speaking of self-regulatory or coping processes, let me offer what I think is an important qualification. We should not expect given self-regulating strategies to be effective in every context. Rather, depending on the environmental demands and options open to the person, some strategies should be serviceable and others not. Frances Cohen and I (1973) found that patients who approached surgery with avoidant strategies, that is, those who did not want to know about their illness and the nature of the surgery, showed a smooth and more rapid post-surgical recovery than did patients adopting a vigilant strategy. We speculated that vigilance might actually be a handicap for the surgical patient because there was nothing constructive he could really do in the postoperative recuperation period except simply to ignore or deny the sources of threat and pain. Trying postoperatively to pay attention vigilantly to every possible cue of danger or sign of discomfort resulted in a longer and more complicated recovery, and this appears to be maladaptive in this situation.

However, a very different strategy seems called for in the stressful context studied by Reuven Gal (1973), namely, seasickness amongst Israeli navy personnel. Holding constant the degree of seasickness, which incidentally can be assessed quite objectively, it was found that sailors who, through personality testing, displayed the trait or disposition to cope in an active, purposive, and vigilant fashion despite being sick, functioned much better at their normal jobs. Forgetting for a moment several possible sources of confounding, such as the measures of coping and the type of population, the juxtaposition of these two studies points up the potential interaction that might exist between the type of coping and the nature of the environmental demands. This suggests the importance of investigating the nature of the environmental demands that interact with coping dispositions and activities.

In closing, let me say that I am inclined to believe that the best strategy for such research on the cognitive mediators of emotion and coping is idiographic and naturalistic rather than nomethetic or normative and experimental. I no longer believe we can learn much by experimentally isolating coping processes, say, or personality variables, or situational demands, from the total context of the individual person in his usual environment. We need to study given classes of normally functioning persons longitudinally, that is, day to day or week to week, as they range from one situational context to another, to analyze and put together effectively the multiple forces to which their emotional reactions respond. I am not rejecting laboratory experiments for many problems, but I am merely questioning their adequacy for the study of emotional processes which are difficult to generate in sufficient intensity with adults in the laboratory setting within the confines of our present-day ethical standards.

Naturalistic research would lack some of the measurement precision and control possible in the laboratory, which is best suited for isolating variables, but it would increase our ability to uncover what has been most lacking in our understanding to date, namely, how the various individual response systems of emotion, and the mediating processes of appraisal and self-regulation, are organized or integrated within the person who is struggling to manage his relations with the environment.

31

REFERENCES

Cohen, F. and Lazarus, R.S. Active coping processes, coping dispositions, and recovery from surgery. *Psychosomatic Medicine*, 1973, *35*, 375-389.

Freud, S. *The problem of anxiety*. New York: Norton, 1936 (also published as *Inhibitions, symptoms and anxiety*).

Gal, R. Coping processes under seasickness conditions. Unpublished manuscript. 1973.

Gray, S.J., Ramsey, C.S., Villarreal, R., and Krakaner, L.J. Adrenal influences upon the stomach and the gastric response to stress. In H. Selye and G. Hansen (Eds.), *Fifth Annual Report on Stress, 1955-1956*. New York: MD Publications, Inc., 1956, p. 138.

Koriat, A., Melkman, R., Averill, J.R., and Lazarus, R.S. The self-control of emotional reactions to a stressful film. *Journal of Personality* 1972, *40*, 601-619.

Lazarus, R.S. *Psychological stress and the coping process*. New York: McGraw-Hill, 1966.

Lazarus, R.S., Averill, J.R., and Opton, E.M., Jr. Towards a cognitive theory of emotion. In Magda B. Arnold (Ed.), *Feelings and Emotions*. New York: Academic Press, 1970, pp. 207-232.

Lazarus, R.S. The self-regulation of emotion. Paper given at symposium entitled Parameters of Emotion, Stockholm, Sweden, June 4-6, 1973.

Lief, H.I., and Fox, R.S. Training for "detached concern" in medical students. In H.I. Lief, V.F. Lief, and N.R. Lief (Eds.), *The psychological basis of medical practice*. New York: Harper & Row, 1963, pp. 12-35.

Mason, J.W. A re-evaluation of the concept of 'non-specificity' in stress theory. *Journal of Psychiatric Research*, 1971, *8*, 323-333.

Mechanic, D. *Students under stress*. New York: The Free Press of Glencoe, 1962.

Skinner, B.F. *Science and human behavior*. New York: Macmillan, 1953.

Symington, T., Currie, A.R., Curran, R.S., and Davidson, J.N. The reaction of the adrenal cortex in conditions of stress. In *Ciba Foundations Colloquia on Endocrinology*. Vol. VIII. *The human adrenal cortex* Little, Brown & Co., 1955, pp. 70-91.

Wolff, C.T., Friedman, S.B., Hofer, M.A., and Mason, J.W., Relationship between psychological defenses and mean urinary 17-hydroxycorticosteriod excretion rates: Parts I and II. *Psychosomatic Medicine*, 1964, *26*, 576-609.

Cognitive Appraisals and Transformations in Self-Control

Walter Mischel[1,2]

Stanford University

The fundamental question motivating the research I will discuss today is how does ideation affect action? How does ideation aid the person to free himself from stimulus control, to generate and maintain difficult behaviors — such as long term work — even when environmental presses make these actions especially difficult? Such a question requires that we try to understand what is happening in the "black box" of the organism and that is just what I would like to do. But, for a behaviorally-oriented experimental psychologist, these attempts to peer into the box require maintenance of the connection between what the individual is doing inside and the observable conditions outside his skin that covary with his private activities.

In our ongoing research my students and I have been trying to develop a methodology for this basic problem that would allow us to investigate experimentally the role of cognitive and attentional processes in self-control. Although my remarks today will focus on that methodology and the findings it has produced in one specific context — delay of gratification or "waiting behavior" — I believe that both the strategy and the results have evident relevance for understanding many aspects of human self-regulation, including the kinds of coping processes discussed by Richard Lazarus in this volume. It should

_____

[1] An abridged version of this paper was presented at the AAAS meetings, February 1974, San Francisco. An extended version of this report appears elsewhere (Mischel, 1974).

[2] The research reported here was supported in part by research grant MH-6830 to Walter Mischel from the National Institute of Health, United States Public Health Service, and Grant GS-32582 from the National Science Foundation.

be plain, therefore, that "delay of gratification" in the present studies serves mainly as the dependent variable. Certainly, voluntary delay is a pervasive, often difficult, and frequently essential human action, but my chief interest here is in the mental activity that permits it and related human self-regulatory behaviors to occur. The research on this topic hopefully will inform us not only about the determinants of waiting but also about the nature of ideation and self-regulation.

To move the cognition-self-control relationship from a rhetorical question into a researchable problem, we began to explore how ideation about relevant, contingent rewards (reinforcers) in a choice situation influences the individual's ability to sustain his goal-directed activity toward the achievement of his preferred outcomes. Given the enormous conceptual weight carried by the notion of reward or "reinforcement" in behavioral psychology, it is remarkable how little is known about the effects of the mental representation of rewards upon the subject's pursuit of them. There seems to be a striking discrepancy between the theoretical significance attributed to rewards for the maintenance of goal-directed behavior and our lack of understanding of how the cognitive or mental representation of rewards figure in the regulation of the complex behaviors that those rewards supposedly "control."

FIRST SPECULATIONS

When we first began to speculate about how attention to the relevant rewards in a contingency might influence voluntary delay for those rewards, there seemed to be few theoretical guides available. A rare exception was Freud's (1911) analysis of the transition from primary to secondary process, which offered one of the few theoretical discussions of how delay of gratification may be bridged. The psychoanalytic formulation suggests that ideation arises initially when there is a block or delay in the process of direct gratification discharge (Rapaport, 1967, p. 315). Freud hypothesized that during such externally imposed delay, the child constructs a "hallucinatory wish-fulfilling image" of the need-satisfying object. Because of frequent association of tension reduction with goal objects, and the development of greater ego organization, the imposed delay of satisfying objects gradually results in the substitution of hallucinatory satisfactions and other thought processes that convert "free cathexes" into "bound cathexes" (e.g., Freud, 1911; Singer, 1955). But, unfortunately, the exact process remains cloudy, in spite of considerable psychoanalytic theorizing about the role of the mental representation of blocked gratifications for the development of delay.

In a second theoretical direction, it seems plausible that "time-binding" (the capacity to bridge delay of gratification) might depend on self-instructional processes through which the person enhances the salience of the delayed consequences of his behavior. One might expect, from that viewpoint, that any factors (situational or within the individual) that make delayed consequences more vivid should facilitate impulse control. While such a view focuses on the self-instructional components of attention to delayed outcomes, it also implies covert self-reinforcement processes through which the individual may strengthen his own delay behavior by vividly anticipating some of the rewarding consequences to which his waiting will lead. Finally, one could also expect that young children would easily forget the deferred outcomes for which they are waiting and therefore stop waiting unless they are reminded of the relevant contingencies and rewards during the delay period.

The above speculations all suggest that conditions that help the person to attend mentally to the delayed reward for which he is waiting should help him to maintain the delay. These speculations would suggest that any cues that make the delayed gratifications more salient, vivid, or immediate (for example, by letting the person look at them, by picturing them in imagination, or by thinking of the object for which he is waiting) should enhance waiting behavior. These anticipations also seem consistent with findings from previous research on choice of immediate smaller versus delayed but larger rewards (Mahrer, 1956; Mischel & Metzner, 1962; Mischel & Staub, 1965; Mischel, 1966). These earlier investigations indicated that an important determinant of choice preference for delayed rewards is the person's expectation ("trust") that he will really get the delayed (but more valuable) outcome.[3] When the child can always see the relevant rewards fewer doubts might arise about their ultimate availability than when the rewards are hidden from view. Therefore, conditions in which the delayed gratification are visible may increase the individual's willingness to wait by increasing his subjective expectancy that the delayed outcome will really still be there at the conclusion of the delay time.

Given these considerations, one might predict that voluntary delay behavior is enhanced when the individual converts the delayed object into more concrete form by making it psychologically more immediate, as by providing himself with representations or physical cues about it. To test that notion, the most direct way to increase the salience of the deferred outcomes and to focus attention on them would be to have them physically present in front of the subject so that he can attend to them vividly and easily. To explore how attention to delayed and immediate outcomes influences waiting behavior, in one study we varied the availability of those outcomes for attention during the delay period (Mischel & Ebbesen, 1970).

---

[3]Note that the present report focuses only on the cognitive conditions that influence the ability to sustain voluntary delay behavior after the subject has chosen to wait; the determinants of the *choice* of immediate versus delayed gratification has been conceptualized in an expectancy-value framework and research relevant to such choice is summarized elsewhere (Mischel, 1974).

ATTENTION TO THE REWARDS REDUCES DELAY

A paradigm was required in which very young children would be willing to stay in an experimental room, waiting by themselves for at least a short time without becoming excessively upset (Mischel & Ebbesen, 1970). As a first step (after the usual play periods for rapport-building), each child was taught a "game" in which he could immediately summon the experimenter by a simple signal. This procedure was practiced until the child obviously understood that he could immediately end his waiting period alone in the room by signalling for the experimenter. The latter always returned immediately from outside the door when the child signalled. The child was then introduced to the relevant contingency. Specifically, he was shown two objects (e.g., snack food treats), one of which he clearly preferred (as determined by pretesting). But to get the preferred object he had to wait for it until the experimenter returned "by himself." However, the child was free throughout this delay period to signal anytime for the experimenter to return. If he signalled he could have the less preferred object at once but would forego the more desirable one later.

To manipulate systematically the degree to which children could attend to the rewards while they were waiting, the reward objects were available to the child's view in all combinations, creating four conditions with respect to the objects available for attention. The children in one condition waited with both the immediate (less preferred) and the delayed (more preferred) rewards facing them in the experimental room so that they could attend to both outcomes. In a second group neither reward was available for the child's attention, both rewards having been removed from his sight. In the remaining two groups either the delayed reward only or the immediate reward only was left facing the child and available for attention while he waited. The length of time before each child voluntarily terminated the waiting period was the dependent measure.

The initial theorizing about delay behavior led us to predict results which were the direct opposite of the ones we found. We had expected that attention to the delayed rewards in the choice situation while waiting would facilitate delay behavior. We found, instead, that attention to the rewards significantly and dramatically decreased delay of gratification. The children waited longest when *no* rewards faced them during the delay period; they waited significantly less long when they faced the delayed reward, or the immediate reward, or both rewards, as Figure 1 indicates, with no significant differences between the reward conditions but a trend for the shortest delay when facing both rewards.

To explore what caused these unexpected results, we tried to see just what the children were doing while they were waiting. Therefore, we observed them closely by means of a one-way mirror throughout the delay period as they sat waiting for their preferred outcomes in what had proved to be the most difficult situation, i.e., with both the immediate and delayed outcomes facing them.

36

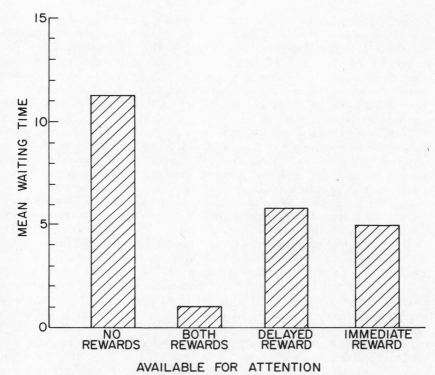

FIG. 1. *Mean minutes of voluntary waiting time for the delayed reward in each attention condition (from Mischel & Ebbesen, 1970).*

These observations were helped by "Mr. Talk Box," a device that consisted of a tape recorder and a microphone that announced its name to the youngster and cheerfully said, "Hi, I have big ears and I love it when children fill them with all the things they think and feel, no matter what." Thereafter, Mr. Talk Box adopted a Rogerian non-directive attitude and acceptingly "uhemed" and "ahad" to whatever the child said to him. In fact, many children seemed to quickly treat Mr. Talk Box as an extension of their psyche and engaged in elaborate, animated discussions with themselves.

Extensive observations of the children during the delay period gradually gave some clues about the mechanisms through which they seemed to mediate and facilitate their own goal-directed waiting. The most effective delay strategies employed by some children were remarkably simple. These youngsters seemed able to wait for the preferred reward for long periods apparently by converting the aversive waiting situation into a more pleasant nonwaiting one. They seemed to manage this by elaborate self-distraction techniques through which they spent their time psychologically doing almost anything other than waiting. Instead of focusing their attention on the rewards, they avoided them. Some of these children covered their eyes with their hands, rested their heads on their arms, and discovered other similar techniques for averting their eyes from the rewards. Many children also seemed to try to reduce the frustration of delay of reward by generating their own distractions: they talked quietly to themselves, sang ("This is such a pretty day, hurray"), created games with their hands and feet, and when all other distractions seemed exhausted even tried to go to sleep during the waiting situation — as one child successfully did, falling into a deep slumber in front of the signal bell. These tactics, of course, are familiar to anyone who has ever been trapped in a boring lecture.

Our observations of the children seem consistent with theorizing which emphasizes the aversiveness of frustration and delayed rewards. If the subject is experiencing conflict and frustration about wanting to end the delay but not wanting to lose the preferred, delayed outcome, then cues that enhance attention to the elements in the conflict (i.e., the two sets of rewards) should increase the aversiveness of waiting. More specifically, when the child attends to the immediate reward his motivation for it increases and he becomes tempted to take it, but is frustrated because he knows that taking it now prevents his getting the more preferred reward later. When the subject attends to the preferred but delayed outcome he becomes increasingly frustrated because he wants it more now but cannot have it yet. When attention is focused on both objects, both of these sources of frustration occur and further delay becomes most aversive; hence, the child terminates quickly (as indeed happened). This reasoning would suggest that conditions that decrease attention to the rewards in the choice contingency and that distract the person (through internal or overt activity) from the conflict and the frustrative delay would make it less aversive to continue goal-directed waiting and thus permit longer delay of gratification. That is, just as cognitive avoidance may help one to cope with anxiety, so may it help to deal with such other aversive events as the frustration of waiting for a desired but delayed outcome and the continuous conflict of whether or not to terminate.

COGNITIVE DISTRACTION HELPS DELAY

The foregoing theorizing suggests that delay of gratification and frustration tolerance should be facilitated by conditions that help the individual to transform the aversive waiting period into a more pleasant nonwaiting situation. Such a transformation could be achieved by converting attention and thoughts away from the frustrative components of delay of gratification. Thus, voluntary delay of reward should be enhanced by any overt or covert activities that serve as distractors from the rewards and thus from the aversiveness of the situation. By means of such distraction, the person should convert the frustrative delay-of-reward situation into a less aversive one. Motoric activities as well as internal cognitions and fantasy which could distract the individual from the reward objects therefore should increase the length of time which he would delay gratification for the sake of getting the preferred outcome.

The crucial requirement here would be to manipulate the child's cognitions. But how can one influence what the child is going to think about? After many poor starts we realized, at last, that our young subjects really might not be basically different from us and thus were capable of following diverse instructions – including instructions to ideate about marshmallows, or pretzels, or fun things that might distract them. We quickly discovered that even at age three or four our subjects could give us elaborate, dramatic examples of the many events that made them feel happy, like finding frogs, or singing, or swinging on a swing with mommy pushing. In turn, we instructed them to think about those fun things while they sat waiting alone for their preferred outcomes. In some of these studies the immediate and delayed rewards were physically not available for direct attention during the waiting period. We manipulated the children's attention to the absent rewards cognitively by different types of instructions given before the start of the delay period. The results showed that cognitions directed toward the rewards substantially reduced, rather than enhanced, the duration of time which the children were able to wait. Thus, attentional and cognitive mechanisms which enhance the salience of the rewards greatly decreased the length of voluntary delay time. In contrast, overt or covert distractions from the rewards (e.g., by prior instructions to think about fun things) facilitated delay of gratification (Mischel, Ebbesen & Zeiss, 1972), as Figure 2 illustrates.

The overall results undermine theories that predict mental attention to the reward objects will enhance voluntary delay by facilitating "time binding" and tension discharge (through cathexes of the image of the object). The data also undermine any "salience" theories which would suggest that making the outcomes salient by imagery, cognitions, and self-instructions about the consequences of delay behavior should increase voluntary delay. The findings unequivocally contradict theoretical expectations that images and cognitions relevant to the gratifications sustain delay behavior. Instead, either looking at the rewards or thinking about them in their absence decreases voluntary delay of gratification. Effective delay thus seems to depend on suppressive and avoidance mechanisms to reduce frustration during the delay period; it does not appear to be mediated by consummatory fantasies about the rewards.

The present results suggest that the person can delay most effectively for a chosen deferred gratification if during the delay period he shifts his attention from the relevant gratifications and occupies himself internally with cognitive distractions. Situational or self-induced cognitions that shift attention from the reward objects appear to facilitate voluntary waiting times appreciably. In order to bridge the delay effectively it is as if the child must make an internal notation of what he is waiting for, perhaps remind himself of it periodically, but spend the remaining time attending to other less frustrative internal and external stimuli, thereby transforming the noxious into the easy and thus taking the thinking and the worrying out of waiting and "will power."

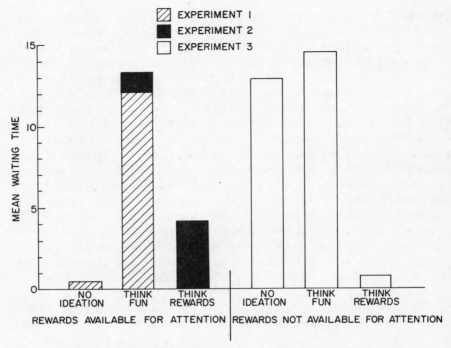

FIG. 2. *Mean minutes of voluntary waiting time for treatment conditions in experiements 1, 2, and 3, comparing different ideation instructions with controls (from Mischel, Ebbesen, & Zeiss, 1972).*

The conclusion that aversive stimuli are avoided cognitively may be restricted to paradigms in which the person believes that thinking about the aversive stimulus cannot change the contingencies in the situation. In contrast, when the aversive stimulus (such as an electric shock) can be avoided, subjects may tend to become vigilant, correctly perceiving the stimulus more quickly than do controls (e.g., Dulany, 1957; Rosen, 1954). That is, when people can potentially control painful events perhaps they think about them more and become vigilantly alert to them. To the extent that the delay-of-gratification situation produces an aversive frustration effect, people are likely to delay better if they avoid ideating about the rewards, but perhaps only if their own behavior during delay cannot affect the time at which the frustration will be terminated. Whether people react to potentially frustrative or painful stimuli by trying to avoid them cognitively or by becoming vigilantly alert to them thus may depend in part on what they can do to control them. We are now exploring these possibilities in ongoing research.

In sum, the findings up to this point thus suggest that the capacity to sustain self-imposed delay of reinforcement depends on the degree to which the individual avoids (or transforms) cues about the frustrativeness of the delay situation — such as cues that remind him of what he expects and wants but is prevented (interrupted, blocked, delayed) from getting. This hypothesis would apply equally to the externally-imposed delays or interruptions that characterize "frustration" and to the self-imposed delay behavior that marks "self-control." To increase subjective frustration, a person then would have to focus cognitively on the goal objects (e.g., by engaging covertly in anticipatory goal responses); to decrease frustration he would have to suppress the goal objects by avoiding them cognitively. In the delay paradigm, "frustration tolerance" would depend on the subject's ability to suppress his attention to the blocked rewards while remaining in the frustrative situation until the goal is attained.

Although the present interpretation seems reasonable, close observation of the children's behavior while they engaged in voluntary delay indicates that it may be both incomplete and too simple. Sheer suppression or distraction from the frustrativeness of the situation seems to be one important determinant of frustration tolerance, but it is unlikely to be the only one. Observation of the children's actions and verbalizations while waiting suggested that those who waited effectively were also engaged in complex self-instructions and internal activities (Mischel, Ebbesen & Zeiss, 1972).

During earlier studies it was noted, for example, that while the child was waiting for the delayed outcome he would often repeat the contingency aloud to himself (alone in the empty room): "If I wait I get..." (naming the more preferred object), "...but if I ring the bell I get..." (naming the less preferred). To maintain his delay behavior effectively, it appeared as if he made an internal notation of what he was waiting for (possibly reminding himself of it by repeating the contingency from time to time), and also reminded himself of the alternative consequences of continuing to delay or of terminating the delay. Intermittently, when not so occupied, he would spend his time distracting himself from the frustrativeness of the delay situation (e.g., by singing to himself), thus transforming the noxious delay into a more pleasant activity. Often it seemed as if the subject also supported his own delay behavior by covert self-reinforcement for waiting. Thus, many children performed diverse covert self-congratulatory reactions as they continued to sustain their goal-directed waiting, and created special subjective contingencies of their own. For example, "If I just wait a little more I'll get it for sure — yes, he'll come back soon now — I'm sure he will, he must."

In view of the extremely complex cognitive activity that seems to mediate delay behavior, it becomes important to consider and control more precisely the covert activities of the subject during the waiting period. The most relevant condition for further study is the one in which the subject is attending cognitively to the reward objects although the rewards are physically absent. In his formulation of delay of gratification, Freud (1911) suggested that delay capacity begins when the child develops images (mental representations) of the delayed reward in the absence of the object itself. According to that view, the hungry infant may gain some satisfaction by forming a "hallucinatory" image of the mother's breast when she is physically unavailable. Recall that to explore this idea Mischel, Ebbesen and Zeiss (1972) had tried to structure some situations in the delay of gratification paradigm in which children would generate images about the absent rewards. Therefore, some children had been instructed (before the start of the delay period) that they might wish to think about the rewards while they actually waited for them. After these instructions the subjects were left alone during the delay period with the physical rewards removed from their visual field. But although such instructions to "think" about the rewards had strong effects, they give us little control over the child's subsequent ideation and attention during the delay period. Unfortunately, the child's cognitive activity during the delay period itself remained unclear.

SYMBOLICALLY PRESENTED REWARDS (IMAGES) HAVE OPPOSITE EFFECTS

While it had been possible to manipulate attention to the actual rewards by varying their presence or absence in the child's visual field (Mischel & Ebbesen, 1970), how could one manipulate the availability of an *image* of the relevant objects when they were absent physically? A study by Mischel and Moore (1973a) approximated this condition, at least roughly, by *symbolic* presentations of the absent objects during the delay period. For this purpose subjects were exposed to slide-presented images of the absent reward objects while waiting for them. The design compared the effect on delay behavior of exposure to images of the "relevant" objects (i.e., the rewarding outcomes for which the subject was waiting) with exposure to images of similar objects that were irrelevant to the delay contingency.

The most important result of the Mischel and Moore (1973a) study was that, to our surprise, exposure to symbolically-presented rewards during the delay period substantially increased (rather than decreased) delay of gratification. This effect of exposure to reward-relevant images is directly opposite to the finding that visual exposure to the rewards themselves greatly decreases delay time (Mischel & Ebbesen, 1970; Mischel, Ebbesen & Zeiss, 1972). These earlier results had been obtained in essentially the same subject population (that is, preschool children in the same nursery school), and from a basically similar delay paradigm. Yet the Mischel and Moore study demonstrated that exposure to images of the relevant rewards enhanced delay behavior more than did exposure to comparable distractions (images of similar but reward-irrelevant objects and blank slides). The crucial difference between the reward-relevant attention manipulations in the earlier experiments and in the present one is that previously children had been exposed to the actual reward objects, but in this study they were exposed to symbolically-presented *images* of the rewards. We must therefore conclude that while attention to the rewards themselves decreases delay behavior, attention to the symbolically presented rewards (i.e., images) increases delay behavior.

TWO FUNCTIONS OF REWARDS?

This pattern of findings may be related to two different functions of reinforcing (rewarding) stimuli that, in turn, may have completely different effects on self-control behavior. Extrapolating from Berlyne's (1960) and Estes' (1972) distinctions, a stimulus may have a motivational (consummatory, arousal) function and an informational (cue) function. The actual reward stimuli (i.e., the real objects) probably have a more powerful motivational effect than do their symbolic representations (i.e., slide images); the latter, however, probably have a more abstract cue function. Seeing the actual goal objects increases the subject's motivation for them, while a picture of the rewards serves to remind him of them but with less affective arousal. The motivational arousal created by attention to the rewards themselves is frustrative because it increases the subject's desire to make the blocked consummatory responses appropriate to the outcome (e.g., eat it, play with it). This arousal function of the real stimulus increases the frustration effect (because the subject cannot let himself make the consummatory response), thus leading to decreased delay, as previously indicated (Mischel, Ebbesen & Zeiss, 1972). But the cue (informative) function of the symbolic reward stimulus, in contrast, may function to guide and sustain the person's goal-directed delay behavior. It may do that by serving as a reminder of the contingency in the delay situation (a reminder of what the person will get if he delays) without being so real as to be frustrative.

In sum, exposure to the reward stimuli themselves may lead the subject to become excessively aroused. This arousal is frustrative because it makes him ready to perform the terminal response in a situation in which he cannot do so, and therefore decreases his ability to continue to delay further. But exposure to the *symbolic* representations of the objects in the form of images (i.e., on the slides) may preserve the cue functions of the rewards while reducing their arousal function. The "image" of the objects may serve more like an abstract "token" or a reminder to sustain delay behavior while the presence of the objects themselves arouses frustration and therefore prevents effective self-control.

We must, however, also consider another fact. When the children were encouraged (by instructions) to ideate about the rewards in their absence, their delay times were as short as when they were exposed to the actual rewards (Mischel, Ebbesen & Zeiss, 1972). Hence, the representation of reward objects by means of instruction-induced thoughts reduces delay behavior, but externally-presented symbolic representation (pictures) of the objects enhances delay of gratification, at least in young children. In response to instructions to think about the rewards the children behaved, in a sense, as if their thoughts were real and as if they could consume them. That is, ideating about the objects had the same effect as looking at them, and in both instances interfered with effective delay of gratification in these subjects. But exposure to pictures of the objects facilitated delay.

COGNITIVE TRANSFORMATIONS OF THE STIMULUS

The total data on attention and imagery in self-control so far indicate that the mode of presentation of the reward stimuli has extremely significant effects. These effects presumably occur because the different modes of presentation lead the subject to ideate about the rewards in different ways. Both the actual objects and instructions to think about them seem to produce consummatory ideation and frustrative arousal, but their symbolic representation may lead the subject to respond to them in a more abstract, nonconsummatory fashion. The effects of attention to the rewards upon delay behavior thus probably depend on *how* the subject attends to them rather than simply on whether or not he does. In that case, if attention is focused at the nonconsummatory (more abstract, informative) cue properties of the reward stimuli, delay behavior should be facilitated. In contrast, attention to the motivational or arousing qualities of the rewards should increase the frustrativeness of delay and interfere with effective self-control. If Freud's (1911) conceptualization of the positive role of the "hallucinatory image" of the blocked gratification in the development of delay of gratification refers to the motivational properties of the image, he was probably incorrect. But if his formulation refers to the nonconsummatory, more abstract cue properties of the image it may still prove to be of value.

To test these theoretical possibilities, our most recent studies have been exploring how the impact of attention to the rewards in the delay paradigm can be modified by the specific *cognitive transformations* which the subject performs with regard to them. In these studies, just before the start of the delay period children are given brief instructions designed to encourage them to ideate in different ways during the actual delay time. For example, one study compared the effects of instructions to ideate about the motivational (consummatory) qualities of the "relevant" rewards with comparable instructions to ideate about their nonmotivational (nonconsummatory) qualities and associations (Mischel & Baker, 1974). The same two types of instructions also were used for the "irrelevant" rewards. "Relevant" and "irrelevant" were operationalized as in the Mischel and Moore (1973a) study. All children had to wait while facing the relevant rewards in the contingency.

44

We found that through instructions the child can cognitively transform the reward objects that face him during the delay period in ways that either permit or prevent effective delay of gratification. If the child has been instructed to focus cognitively on the consummatory qualities of the relevant reward objects (such as the pretzel's crunchy, salty taste or the chewy, sweet, soft taste of the marshmallows), then it becomes difficult for him to wait. Conversely, if he cognitively transforms the stimulus to focus on nonconsummatory qualities (by thinking about the pretzel sticks, for example, as long, thin, brown logs, or by thinking about the marshmallows as white, puffy clouds or as round, white moons), he can wait for long time periods (Mischel & Baker, 1974). The main results are shown in Table 1.

TABLE 1.
*Mean delay time in each ideation instruction condition
(from Mischel & Baker, 1974)*[a]

Rewards in Ideation	Content of Ideation	
	Consummatory	Nonconsummatory
Relevant[b]	5.60	13.51
Irrelevant[b]	16.82	4.46

[a]Maximum possible delay time is 20 minutes. All subjects facing the rewards. Data are in minutes.

[b]To contingency in the waiting situation.

Most interesting, transformations of the reward objects that focus on their nonconsummatory qualities provide more than mere cognitive distraction. The Mischel and Baker study compared, in this regard, the effects of instructions that focus on nonconsummatory qualities of the relevant reward objects (i.e., those for which the subject is actually waiting) with the same instructions for irrelevant rewards. When the children had been instructed to ideate about nonconsummatory qualities of the relevant rewards, their mean delay time was more than 13 minutes (20 minutes was the maximum possible). In contrast, when subjects had been given the same instructions with regard to the irrelevant rewards (i.e., comparable but not in the delay contingency), their average delay time was less than 5 minutes. Thus, attention to the nonconsummatory qualities and associations of the actual reward objects in the delay contingency substantially enhances the ability to wait for them, and it does so more effectively than when the same ideation instructions focus on comparable objects irrelevant to the delay contingency.

One might argue that the relatively low delay time obtained when instructions dealt with ideation for the "irrelevant" rewards reflects that young children simply have trouble thinking about reward objects that are not present. Note, however, that the longest mean delay time (almost 17 minutes) occurred when subjects were instructed to ideate about those same objects but with regard to their consummatory qualities (see Table 1). This finding also is provocative theoretically. It suggests that while consummatory ideation about a potentially available object makes it difficult to delay gratification, similar consummatory ideation about an outcome that is simply unattainable in the situation (i.e., the "irrelevant" rewards), rather than being aversive, is highly pleasurable and may serve to sustain prolonged delay behavior. That is, consummatory ideation about reward objects that are not expected and not available in the delay contingency (the irrelevant rewards) may serve as an interesting, effective distractor, hence facilitating waiting. In contrast, similar ideation about the relevant but blocked rewards heightens the frustration of wanting what one expects but cannot yet have. By making the delay more aversive, the length of time that one continues to wait is reduced.

Further support for the powerful role of cognitive transformations in delay behavior comes from several other studies. A follow-up of the Mischel and Moore (1973a) experiment replicated the original finding that exposure to slides of the relevant rewards leads to significantly longer delay than does exposure to slides of the comparable rewards that are irrelevant to the delay contingency (Mischel & Moore, 1973b). The same study also showed that the delay-enhancing effects of the relevant slides can be completely wiped out when subjects are instructed (before the delay interval) to ideate about the consummatory qualities of the relevant rewards while waiting for them.

Our studies on cognitive transformation also have implications for earlier research under the label "cognitive appraisal." Previous research on "cognitive appraisal" has investigated how the cognitive appraisal of threatening stimuli (a film of crude, primitive genital operations) influences emotional responses to those stimuli (Speisman, Lazarus, Mordkoff & Davison, 1964). The findings showed that emotional responses were higher when the film was accompanied by a sound track that emphasized the dangers of such an operation as opposed to sound tracks that denied such dangers or "intellectualized" them in a detached manner. The authors of this widely cited, interesting study interpreted their results as due to differences in "cognitive appraisal" generated by the different sound tracks. The present research (e.g., Mischel & Baker, 1974) provides a more direct demonstration of the importance of cognitive appraisal because the stimulus situation remained identical across situations: all children faced the identical rewards. (In the Speisman et al. study, in contrast, different sound tracks accompanied the film, thus creating different stimulus conditions.) The present work provides a method of manipulating cognitive appraisal more directly by means of instructions through which subjects may transform the identical stimuli into diverse cognitive representations.

46

Through instructions the children can easily transform the real objects (present in front of them) into an abstract version (a "color picture in your head"), or they can transform the picture of the objects (presented on a slide projected on a screen in front of them) into the "real" objects by pretending in imagination that they are actually there on a plate in front of them. Specifically, Mischel and Moore (1973b) exposed preschool subjects either to a slide-presented image of the rewards or to the actual rewards. In each of these conditions half the children were instructed before the start of the delay period to imagine a "picture" of the reward objects during the delay period. For example:

> ... Close your eyes. In your head try to see the picture of the _____(immediate and delayed rewards). Make a color picture of (them); put a frame around them. You can see the picture of them. Now open your eyes and do the same thing. (more practice) ... From now on you can see a picture that shows _____(immediate and delayed rewards) here in front of you. The _____ aren't real; they're just a picture ...
> When I'm gone remember to see the picture in front of you.

Conversely, half the children in each of the conditions were instructed before the delay period (with similar techniques) to imagine the *real* rewards actually present in front of them while waiting. Details of the instructions were adapted to make them plausible in each condition and a maximum delay time of 20 minutes was possible. The results indicated that the crucial determinant of delay behavior was the subject's cognitive representation, regardless of what was actually in front of the child. When imagining the rewards as a picture, the mean delay time was almost 18 minutes regardless of whether the real rewards or a picture of them actually faced the child. But when representing the rewards cognitively as if they were real, subjects' delay time was significantly and very substantially lower, regardless of whether the slide or the actual set of rewards was objectively in front of them (see Table 2).

TABLE 2.
Mean delay time as a function of cognitive transformations (from Mischel & Moore, 1973b)[a]

Objectively Facing Subject	Cognitive Representation of Rewards as:	
	Pictures	Real
Picture of Rewards	17.75	5.95
Real Rewards	17.70	7.91

[a]Maximum possible delay time is 20 minutes. Data are in minutes.

In sum, our overall findings on cognitive stimulus transformations clearly reveal that how children represent the rewards cognitively (not what is physically in front of them) determines how long they delay gratification. Regardless of the stimulus in their visual field, if they imagine the real objects as present they cannot wait very long for them. But if they imagine pictures (abstract representations) of the objects they can wait for long time periods (and even longer than when they are distracting themselves with abstract representations of objects that are comparable but not relevant to the rewards for which they are waiting). By means of instructions (given before the child begins to wait) about what to imagine during the delay period, it is possible to completely alter (in fact, to reverse) the effects of the physically present reward stimuli in the situation and to cognitively control delay behavior with substantial precision. While arousal-generating cognitions about the real objects in the contingency significantly impede delay, cognitions about their nonconsummatory (nonmotivational) qualities or about their abstract representations enhance delay.

Thus, *how* the subject ideates about the outcomes (rather than whether or not he does) appears to be crucial. In the delay paradigm, cognitive representations of the rewards (goals, outcomes) that emphasize their motivational (consummatory, arousal) qualities, we suggest, prevent effective delay by generating excessive frustration, at least in young children. The more the subject focuses on the arousing qualities of the blocked goals, the more intense and aversive the choice conflict and the delay become and the sooner he terminates the situation. Conversely, cognitive representation of the same objects that focuses on their nonconsummatory (more abstract, less arousing) qualities appears to facilitate the maintenance of goal-directed behavior.

In future research it will be important to explore the exact mechanisms that underlie this facilitation. It seems likely that abstract cognitive representations of the rewards permit the subject to remind himself of the contingency and to engage in self-reinforcement for further delay without becoming debilitatingly aroused and frustrated. But the specific processes require further study. Hopefully, such work will continue to clarify not only the mechanisms in delay of gratification but also how the mental representation of goal objects ("rewards") motivates and guides complex waiting and working.

The present studies have demonstrated that the specific ways in which rewards are represented cognitively, rather than their physical presence or absence, determine the impact of those rewards on the subject's ability to control his behavior in pursuit of them. My students and I now are moving in several new directions aimed at studying self-regulation from somewhat different, hopefully complementary, vantage points. In one direction we are examining how the child's "plans" help him to avoid frustration and to persist in goal-directed activity even in the face of temptations and distractions. In a second direction, we are investigating the types of stimuli to which children prefer to be exposed while working or waiting for delayed gratification. The results here should tell us how well (and whether or not) the children themselves know and follow the "rules" governing the effects of reward-relevant ideation on delay behavior. These and related efforts hopefully will lead to a more complete glimpse of the mechanisms and "person variables" through which human beings may achieve increasing control over their environment and over their own behavior (Mischel, 1973).

REFERENCES

Berlyne, D. *Conflict, arousal and curiosity*. New York: McGraw-Hill, 1960.

Dulany, D.E., Jr. Avoidance learning of perceptual defense and vigilance. *Journal of Abnormal and Social Psychology*, 1957, *55*, 333-338.

Estes, W.K. Reinforcement in human behavior. *American Scientist*, 1972, *60*, 723-729.

Freud, S. Formulations regarding the two principles in mental functioning. (1911) In *Collected papers*, Vol. 4. New York: Basic Books, 1959.

Mahrer, A.R. The role of expectancy in delayed reinforcement. *Journal of Experimental Psychology*, 1956, *52*, 101-106.

Mischel, W. Theory and research on the antecedents of self-imposed delay of reward. In B.A. Maher (Ed.), *Progress in experimental personality research*, Vol. 3. New York: Academic Press, 1966.

Mischel, W. Toward a cognitive social learning reconceptualization of personality. *Psychological Review*, 1973, *80*, 252-283.

Mischel, W. Processes in delay of gratification. In L. Berkowitz (Ed.), *Advances in experimental social psychology*, Vol. 7. New York: Academic Press, 1974.

Mischel, W., & Baker, N. Cognitive transformations of reward objects through instructions. *Journal of Personality and Social Psychology*, 1974, in press.

Mischel, W., & Ebbesen, E.G. Attention in delay of gratification. *Journal of Personality and Social Psychology*, 1970, *16*, 239-337.

Mischel, W., Ebbesen, E.B., & Zeiss, A. Cognitive and attentional mechanisms in delay of gratification. *Journal of Personality and Social Psychology*, 1972, *21*, 204-218.

Mischel, W., & Metzner, R. Preference for delayed reward as a function of age, intelligence, and length of delay interval. *Journal of Abnormal and Social Psychology*, 1962, *64*, 425-431.

Mischel, W., & Moore, B. Effects of attention to symbolically-presented rewards upon self-control. *Journal of Personality and Social Psychology*, 1973, *28*, 172-179. (a)

Mischel, W., & Moore, B. Cognitive transformations of the stimulus in delay of gratification. Unpublished manuscript, Stanford University, 1973. (b)

Mischel, W., & Staub, E. Effects of expectancy on working and waiting for larger rewards. *Journal of Personality and Social Psychology*, 1965, *2*, 625-633.

Rapaport, D. On the psychoanalytic theory of thinking. In M.M. Gill (Ed.), *The collected papers of David Rapaport*. New York: Basic Books, 1967.

Rosen, A.C. Change in perceptual threshold as a protective function of the organism. *Journal of Personality*, 1954, *23*, 182-195.

Singer, J.L. Delayed gratification and ego development: Implications for clinical and experimental research. *Journal of Consulting Psychology*, 1955, *19*, 259-266.

Speisman, J.C., Lazarus, R.S., Mordkoff, A.M., and Davison, L.A. The experimental reduction of stress based on ego-defense theory. *Journal of Abnormal and Social Psychology* 1964, *68*, 367-380.

An Attributional Interpretation of Expectancy-Value Theory

Bernard Weiner[1]

University of California, Los Angeles

For the past several years my colleagues and I have been developing an attributional model of achievement motivation. Although the empirical support for the theory is pretty much confined to achievement-related behaviors, we naturally hope that we are building a motivational model that transcends the achievement domain.

Generally speaking, we have used some of the principles of social perception to broaden the cognitive framework of Expectancy X Value theory. Causal attributions are the cornerstones of our model. Causal attributions in the area of achievement motivation primarily refer to the perceived reasons for success and failure.

THE PERCEIVED CAUSES OF SUCCESS AND FAILURE

Our initial guides in searching for the perceived causes of success and failure were Julian Rotter and, more importantly, Fritz Heider. We postulate that individuals utilize four elements of ascription both to postdict (interpret) and to predict the outcome of an achievement-related event. The four causal elements are ability, effort, task difficulty, and luck. That is, in attempting to explain the prior success or failure of an achievement-related event, the individual assesses his own or the performer's ability level, the amount of effort that was expended, the difficulty of the task, and the magnitude and direction of experienced luck.

---

[1] An extended version of this address appeared in Weiner, B. (Ed.) *Achievement motivation and Attribution Theory*, General Learning Press, 1974. This paper was written while the author was supported by Grant GS 35216 from the National Science Foundation.

51

It is assumed that values are assigned to these elements and that the task outcome is differentially ascribed to the four causal sources. Similarly, future expectations of success and failure are based upon the assumed level of ability in relation to perceived task difficulty, as well as an estimation of intended effort and anticipated luck. There are, of course, other causes of success and failure, such as fatigue, bad mood, teacher bias, and so on. But we have repeatedly found that ability, effort, task difficulty, and luck are the most general and salient of the causes of achievement outcomes.

A Two-Dimensional Analysis

We have comprised the causes of success and failure within a two-dimensional taxonomy (Weiner et al., 1971; Weiner et al., 1972). Ability and effort are properties internal to the person, while task difficulty and luck are external factors. This is the familiar internal-external dimension first proposed by Rotter. In addition, ability and task difficulty are relatively stable or invariant, while luck implies variability and effort may be augmented or decreased from one moment to the next. Thus, the four causes are describable within a 2 x 2 classification scheme (see Table 1).

TABLE 1.
Classification scheme for the perceived determinants of achievement behavior

Stability	Locus of Control	
	Internal	External
Stable	Ability	Task difficulty
Unstable	Effort	Luck

As shown in Table 1, ability is an internal, stable cause; effort is an internal, unstable cause; task difficulty is external and stable; and luck is both external and variable. Some of our more recent work has suggested that intentionality is a third dimension of perceived causality, while interpersonal stability may be a fourth causal dimension. These additional dimensions will be neglected here.

Given a tentative list of causes and a taxonomy, we proceeded in two research directions: backwards to the information, processes, and structures that influence causal decisions, and forwards to the effects of causal judgments on future behavior. I will first very briefly describe some of the antecedents that influence causal judgments, and then I will concentrate my attention upon the behavioral consequences of causal ascriptions.

ANTECEDENTS

Specific Cues

The main antecedent cues for causal judgments are specific information, such as past success history, social norms, pattern of performance, time spent at the task, and so on. For example, ability inferences are primarily determined by past history information. Repeated success or failure in part indicates whether an individual "can" or "cannot." Outcome information considered in conjunction with social norms particularly is used to infer ability level (see Frieze & Weiner, 1971; Weiner & Kukla, 1970). If, for example, one succeeds at a task that all others fail, then he or she is likely to be perceived as very able.

Task difficulty generally is inferred from social norms and from objective task characteristics, such as the steepness of a mountain about to be climbed or the length of a puzzle. But social norms are most heavily weighted in task difficulty judgments. We have consistently found that the greater the percentage of others succeeding at a task, the more likely that a given success will be ascribed to the ease of the task. In a similar manner, the greater the percentage of others failing at a task, the more likely that a given failure will be attributed to the difficulty of the task.

Effort is inferred from a number of observables, such as the time spent at a task and perceived muscular tension. In addition, covariation of outcome with an incentive is likely to produce effort ascriptions.

Finally, luck is inferred from an apparent lack of personal control over the outcome and variability in the outcome sequence. Thus, the number rolled on a die will be ascribed to chance. But repeated appearance of the same number suggests personal control over the outcome and would produce ascriptions to ability.

Individuals can combine and synthesize the various informational cues, such as past success history, social norms, variability in the outcome sequence, and so on, and reach reliable causal judgments (see Frieze & Weiner, 1971; Frieze, 1973).

Causal Schemata

In addition to specific cues, our research indicates that cognitive structures, such as causal schemata, also influence the judgment process. A causal schema is a relatively permanent structure that refers to the belief a person holds about the relationship between an observed event (an effect) and the perceived causes of that event (Kelley, 1972). For example, it may be believed that either high ability *or* hard work will produce success. This disjunctive set of causal relations is referred to as a *sufficient* causal schema. Each cause in and of itself is capable of producing the effect. This schema often is elicited by typical events, such as success at an easy task (Kun & Weiner, 1973). Success at an easy task is perceived as due to high ability *or* hard work. Conversely, it may be believed that both ability *and* effort are required for success. This conjunctive set of causal relations is referred to as a *necessary* causal schema. A necessary schema often is elicited by unusual events, such as success at a difficult task. Success at a difficult task is perceived as requiring both ability *and* effort. Necessary versus sufficient schemata generate disparate perceptions concerning the causes of success and failure.

Individual Predispositions

There are individual differences in causal preferences. Everyday observations suggest, for example, that some individuals readily invoke luck explanations, while others perceive innate or learned ability as the primary determinant of achievement-related success. Our work with individual differences in motivational structures has demonstrated that the motive to strive for success, or what is known as the need for achievement, markedly influences causal ascriptions.

Both correlational and experimental studies have firmly established that individuals classified as high or low in need for achievement have disparate attributional biases (see Weiner et al., 1971). Given success, persons high in achievement motivation perceive that high ability and high effort were the responsible factors. Persons low in achievement needs display no clear attributional preferences for success. On the other hand, given failure, individuals high in achievement needs ascribe the outcome to a lack of effort, while persons low in achievement needs attribute the outcome to a lack of ability. Individual differences in causal biases will be examined in greater detail later in this paper.

Summary

To recap (see Table 2), thus far it has been contended that the causal ascriptions for success and failure include ability, effort, task difficulty, and luck, as well as less common ascriptions such as mood, fatigue, illness, and so on. These causes may be subsumed within two primary and two secondary dimensions, respectively labeled locus of control (internal versus external), stability (fixed versus variable), perceived voluntary control (intentional versus unintentional), and interpersonal stability (fixed versus variable).

The determinants of causal ascriptions are, in part, specific cues such as past outcome history, social norms, pattern of performance, stimulus characteristics of the task, randomness of outcome, and so forth. In addition, causal schemata pertaining to a differentiation between necessary and sufficient causality and individual dispositions in achievement-related needs influence causal ascriptions. These linkages are shown in Table 2. We also have evidence that reinforcement schedules and reinforcement rates also are used to infer causation and that direct information from others influences beliefs about causality. But these research areas are neglected here.

One can see from Table 2 that cognitive processes such as information search, information assembly, and causal attributions, as well as cognitive structures, play important roles in our model. Such cognitive processes and structures have been neglected by expectancy-value theorists.

TABLE 2.
The attribution process for success and failure

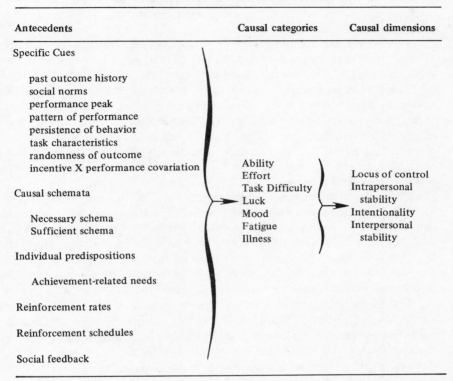

Antecedents	Causal categories	Causal dimensions
Specific Cues		
past outcome history		
social norms		
performance peak		
pattern of performance		
persistence of behavior		
task characteristics		
randomness of outcome		
incentive X performance covariation	Ability	
	Effort	Locus of control
Causal schemata	Task Difficulty	Intrapersonal
	Luck	stability
Necessary schema	Mood	Intentionality
Sufficient schema	Fatigue	Interpersonal
	Illness	stability
Individual predispositions		
Achievement-related needs		
Reinforcement rates		
Reinforcement schedules		
Social feedback		

CONSEQUENCES

I will turn now from this very brief overview of antecedents to the consequences of causal ascriptions. Recall I indicated that one of our goals has been to integrate attribution theory within an Expectancy X Value framework. The manner in which causal ascriptions influence goal expectancies and affect (incentive value) will now be examined.

CAUSAL ATTRIBUTIONS AND GOAL EXPECTANCY

Inasmuch as the concept of expectancy has played such a central role in cognitive approaches to motivation, it is disappointing that its operational linkages and specified antecedents have remained so vague. The first systematic analysis of the determinants of expectancies was undertaken by Tolman (1932). Tolman stated that expectancies of reward are jointly determined by learning capacities and environmental variables. The environmental variables include the frequency and recency of reward. Thus, laws primarily taken from the animal literature and associationistic psychology were used to infer the strength of a goal expectancy.

Surprisingly, the inferred determinants of expectancy and expectancy shifts as deduced from research on humans are even less satisfying. Investigators in the achievement area have not systematically examined the antecedents of the expectancy (subjective probability) of success. Expectancy is typically manipulated by merely telling subjects their chances of success. To a lesser extent, probabilities have been manipulated by varying past success history, the number of persons against whom one is competing, or the objective difficulty of the task (see Weiner, 1970). The only determinants of expectancy shifts that have been identified are success and failure. Following success expectancy generally rises while after failure it usually drops ("typical" shifts).

Our research shows that causal ascriptions for success and failure in part determine the direction and the magnitude of expectancy shifts. For example, failure that is ascribed to low ability should decrease the expectancy of future goal attainment more than failure that is ascribed to bad luck, fatigue, or mood. In a similar manner, success ascribed to good luck should result in a lesser increment in the subjective expectancy of future success at that task than success ascribed to high ability or to the ease of the task.

The general relationships between expectancy shifts and causal ascriptions are depicted in Figure 1. The figure shows that ascriptions of an outcome to stable factors produce greater typical shifts in expectancy than do ascriptions to unstable factors. The differential shifting of expectancies as a function of the stability of the attribution is presumed to occur given either internal (ability versus effort) or external (task difficulty versus luck) causal attributions. However, as shown in Figure 1, attributions to effort produce greater typical shifts than do attributions to luck. This is because effort also has stable characteristics ("He is a lazy person"), and the intent to succeed is likely to remain relatively constant.

Empirical Evidence

The relationships between causal attributions and expectancy shifts shown in Figure 1 have been tested in five experiments (Fontaine, 1974; McMahon, 1973; Meyer, 1970; Nierenberg, Goldstein & Weiner, in press; and Rosenbaum, 1972). All these investigations yield strong corroborative evidence. Meyer (1970; reported, in part, in Weiner et al., 1972) performed the prototype experiment. Meyer had subjects either repeatedly succeed or repeatedly fail at a digit-symbol substitution task. Following each trial causal ascriptions were made to ability, effort, task difficulty, and luck. The ascriptions were constrained to total 100%. In addition, subjective expectancy of success was reported for the next trial. The

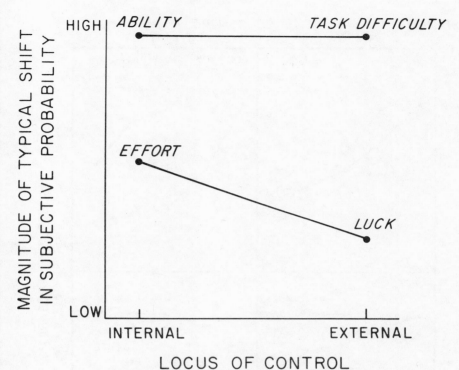

FIG. 1. *Hypothesized relationships between causal attributions for success and failure and the magnitude of typical expectancy shifts (increments in expectancy after a success and decrements in expectancy after a failure).*

data clearly revealed that in the failure condition the subjective expectancies were lower when attributions were predominantly to low ability and a hard task rather than to a lack of effort or bad luck (see Figure 2). In sum, attributions to the stable elements augment typical expectancy shifts while attributions to the unstable elements reduce the magnitude of typical expectancy changes. Figure 3, which shows the expectancy changes as a function of the attributions to stable vs unstable elements, reveals that expectancies shift only slightly downward following failure if causal ascriptions are made to unstable, rather than to stable, factors.

Rotter (1966) previously has contended that typical expectancy shifts are minimized when reinforcements are perceived as externally controlled (chance situations), and maximized when reinforcements are perceived as internally controlled (skill situations). Examination of Table 1 in this paper reveals that skill (ability) versus chance (luck) perceptions of causality differ not only in locus of control but also in their degree of stability. One's skill is relatively

57

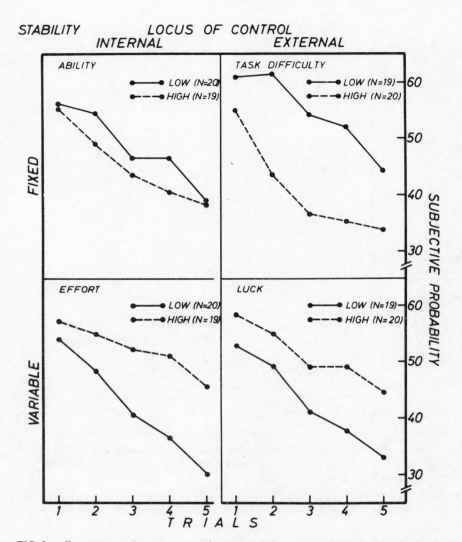

FIG. 2. *Expectancy of success as a function of above versus below median ascription to the four causal elements. High ascription indicates that a lack of ability, a difficult task, lack of effort, and bad luck are the perceived causes of failure. (From Weiner, Heckhausen, Meyer & Cook, 1972, p. 243).*

stable, while luck is variable. Hence, comparisons of expectancy shifts between tasks that elicit skill versus chance perceptions of responsibility confound two dimensions of causality. This makes it impossible to determine whether the differential expectancy shifts are to be attributed to differences in locus of

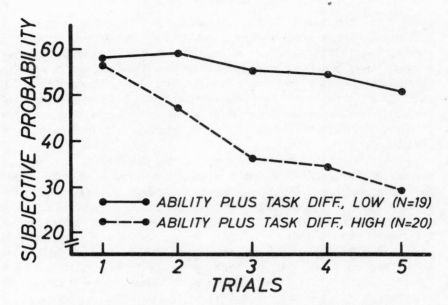

FIG. 3. Expectancy of success as a function of above versus below median ascription to the fixed attributional elements (corresponds respectively to below versus above median ascription to effort plus luck). (From Weiner, Heckhausen, Meyer & Cook, 1972, p. 243).

control or to disparate beliefs about stability. Our research, however, as exemplified in the investigation by Meyer, has separated the locus of control from the stability causal dimension. It has been proven that expectancy shifts are unrelated to locus of control, but they are related to the stability of the causal dimension.

A recent study has directly pitted the locus of control versus causal stability explanations of expectancy change. Nierenberg et al. (in press) gave subjects either 0,1,2,3,4, or 5 success experiences at a block-design task. In contrast to the study by Meyer (1970), different subjects were placed in the various experimental conditions. Following the success trial(s), expectancy of success and causal ascriptions were obtained.

Expectancy of future success was determined by having subjects indicate "how many of the next ten similar designs [he] believed that [he] would successfully complete." To assess perceptions of causality, subjects were required to mark four Likert-type scales that were identical with respect to either the stability or locus of control dimensional anchors, but which differed along the alternate dimension. For example, one attribution question was "Did you succeed on this task because you are always good at these kinds of tasks or because you tried especially hard on this particular task?" "Always good" and "tried hard," the anchors on this scale, are identical on the locus of control dimension (internal), but they differ in perceived stability, with ability a stable attribute and effort an unstable cause. In a similar manner, judgments were made between "lucky" and "tried hard" (unstable causes differing in locus of control), "these tasks are always easy" and "lucky" (external causes differing in stability), and "always good" and "always easy" (stable causes differing in locus of control). Thus, the judgments were made *within* a single causal dimension. This permitted a direct test of the locus of control versus stability interpretations of expectancy change.

Table 3 shows the mean expectancy of success judgments for the groups of subjects as a function of the number of success experiences. The table reveals that the expectancy of future success is directly related to the stability of the perceived cause of the prior positive outcome(s). Individuals classified as high in their attribution of success to stable factors have more positive overall expectancies than individuals relatively medium or relatively low in their attribution of success to stable causes. Indeed, within the five experimental conditions there is only one rank-order reversal (in the two-trial condition) in the magnitudes of the expectancy figures. Table 3 also reveals that perceptions of control are not significantly related to the stated expectancies of success.

TABLE 3.
Mean expectancy scores for subjects classified as high (upper third), medium (middle third) and low (lower third) in perceived stability and perceived locus of control

Causal Dimension		0	Number of Successes					
			1	2	3	4	5	$\overline{X}$
Stability								
High			8.43[1]	8.86	8.86	8.86	9.14	8.83
Medium			7.43	6.43	8.57	8.86	8.86	8.03
Low			6.86	7.00	7.86	8.14	8.86	7.74
	$\overline{X}$	7.09[2]	7.57	7.43	8.43	8.62	8.95	8.20
Locus of Control (Internal)								
High			7.71	7.43	8.86	8.71	9.28	8.40
Medium			7.71	7.14	8.14	8.71	8.71	8.08
Low			7.28	7.53	8.28	8.43	8.86	8.08
	$\overline{X}$	7.09	7.57	7.43	8.43	8.62	8.95	8.20

[1] N = 7 in each cell
[2] N = 21

In sum, the results of this study unequivocally support the attributional conception and contradict the predictions from social learning theory. The stability of causal attributions, rather than their locus of control, is related to expectancy of success. The association between the stability of causal factors and the expectancy of success has now been demonstrated in a number of studies. These investigations have used group and individual testing procedures, manipulated success as well as failure, used within- and between-subject experimental designs, and a wide variety of experimental tasks and methods of assessing causal attributions have been employed. In addition, while the designs of the Meyer (1970) and Nierenberg et al. (in press) investigations are correlational, other corroborating studies have manipulated the causal determinants (Fontaine, 1974; Rosenbaum, 1972). The relationship between causal stability and expectancy of success is proven. I find it unfortunate that psychologists continue to discuss locus of control in relation to expectancy of success and continue to confound the internal aspects of perceived control with the volitional and stable dimensions of causality.

CAUSAL ASCRIPTIONS AND AFFECTIVE REACTIONS

Cognitive theories of motivation generally maintain that the intensity of aroused motivation is determined jointly by the expectation that the response will lead to the goal and the attractiveness of the goal object. The greater the perceived likelihood of goal attainment and the greater the incentive value of the goal, the more intense is the presumed degree of positive motivation. It has been shown that goal expectations are markedly influenced by the stability of the perceived causes of success and failure. What, then, is the relationship between causal ascriptions and the incentive value or the affective consequences of goal attainment?

The hypothesized linkages between causal ascriptions and the emotional consequences of success and failure are shown in Figure 4. Figure 4 reveals that pride and shame are maximized when achievement outcomes are ascribed internally and minimized when success and failure are attributed to external causes. Thus, success attributed to high ability or hard work is expected to produce more pride than success that is ascribed to the ease of the task or to good luck. In a similar manner, failure perceived as due to low ability or a lack of effort is expected to result in greater shame than failure that is attributed to a hard task or bad luck. In sum, locus of causality influences the affective consequences of achievement behaviors. In addition, Figure 4 reveals that causal ascriptions to effort, which is an internal cause under volitional control, maximize positive and negative affects for success and failure. Of course, failure ascribed to external factors may produce emotional reactions such as anger or frustration. But external attributions minimize *achievement-related affects* of pride and shame.

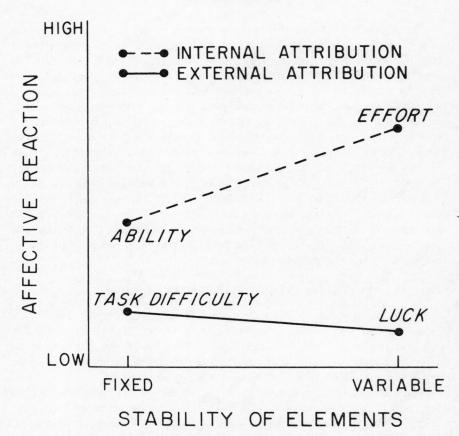

FIG. 4. *Hypothesized relationships between causal attributions for success and failure and the magnitude of achievement-related affects of pride and shame.*

An experimental paradigm has been used with particular success to demonstrate the significant effects of effort attributions on affective responses. Weiner and Kukla (1970) instructed subjects to pretend that they were teachers, evaluating pupils. The subjects received information concerning the hypothetical pupils' level of ability (high or low), effort expenditure (high or low), and their outcome on an exam (excellent, good, borderline, moderate failure, or clear failure). All twenty possible combinations of information (2 levels of ability X 2 levels of effort X 5 levels of outcome) were presented for evaluation. Thus, for example, a student described as high in ability, low in effort, and a moderate failure at the exam was evaluated. The evaluative judgments ranged from +5 (highest reward) to -5 (highest punishment).

The results of this study are shown in Figure 5. The figure reveals a main effect for outcome: good exam performance is rewarded while poor performance is punished. In addition, high effort is positively valued and lack of effort is punished. Finally, pupils low in ability are rewarded more and punished less than those high in ability. Pupils low in ability and high in effort (-AE) therefore receive the highest evaluations. It appears that the overcoming of a personal handicap through hard work is most admired while the failure to utilize one's capacities is most despised. The general pattern of results shown in Figure 5 has been replicated in nine published experiments (Eswara, 1972; Kaplan & Swant, 1973; Rest, Nierenberg, Weiner & Heckhausen, 1973; Weiner & Kukla, 1970; Zander, Fuller & Armstrong, 1972). These replications spanned different cultures (America, India, and Switzerland); different social situations (group versus individual tasks); different levels of task difficulty (easy, medium, or

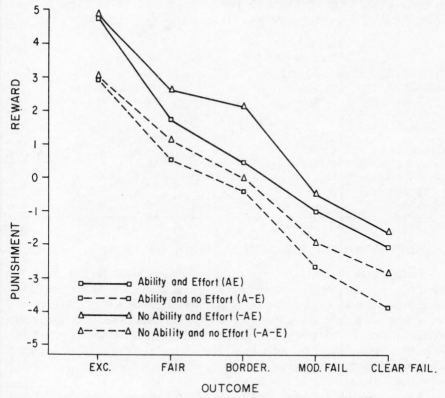

FIG. 5. *Evaluation (reward and punishment) as a function of pupil ability, effort, and examination outcome. (From Weiner and Kukla, 1970, p. 3).*

difficult); self- and other-judgments; and within- as well as between-subject experimental designs.

General Summary

Cognitive theories of motivation specify that performance is a function of the expectancy that the response will lead to the goal and the incentive value of the goal object. It has been established that causal ascriptions influence both goal anticipations and the affective (incentive or reinforcement) consequences of success and failure. Causal stability determines expectancy shifts while locus of control influences affective responses. The general attributional model of achievement strivings partially depicted in Table 2 may now be expanded to include the psychological consequences of both the stability and the locus of control dimensions of causality (see Table 4). Expectancy X Value theory typically includes only the last two columns of the table and thus neglects many important cognitive processes. Elsewhere (Weiner, 1972), I have labeled Expectancy X Value conceptions as quasi-cognitive.

TABLE 4.
An attributional model of achievement motivation

Antecedents	Causal ascriptions	Causal dimensions	Dimensional consequences	Behavioral consequences
Specific cues Individual differences Causal schemata Reinforcement rates Reinforcement schedules	Ability Effort Task difficulty Luck	Stability ⟶ Locus ⟶ of Control	Expectancy shifts Affect	Various indices of performance

CAUSAL ATTRIBUTIONS AND PERFORMANCE

I would now like to present one experiment that spans the entire linkages in the model and demonstrates the effects of causal cognitions on performance. Recall it was previously indicated that individuals high and low in achievement needs have disparate attributions for success and failure and it was also contended that causal ascriptions mediate achievement strivings. It therefore logically follows that if the attributions for success and failure made by the achievement motive groups can be changed, then their achievement-related behaviors also will be altered.

Attributions for failure among individuals differing in achievement needs were experimentally manipulated by Weiner and Sierad (1974). Subjects were given four trials of repeated failure at a digit-symbol substitution task. Prior to the failure, one-half of the subjects were randomly assigned to a drug-attribution condition; the remaining subjects were in a control condition. The subjects in the drug condition were given a placebo pill that allegedly interfered with hand-eye coordination, a skill described as needed for good performance at the substitution task. Hence, personal failure would be ascribed to the drug. In the control condition no attempt was made to alter attributions. Thus, typical low effort and low ability attributions for failure were expected among subjects respectively high or low in achievement needs.

Now consider how Expectancy X Value theory, when combined with attribution theory, leads to predictions in this rather complex experiment. Table 5 outlines the temporal sequence of mediating events and the hypothesized behavioral consequences for subjects low and high in achievement needs in the control and in the pill conditions. Consider first the subjects low in achievement needs. Their bias to attribute personal failure to low ability is altered by the experimental manipulation, for in the experimental condition failure is ascribed to the action of the drug. Both low ability and the drug effects are perceived as stable within the time period of the experiment. Thus, failure should be expected to continue and the expectancy of success is assumed to be equally low in both conditions. But the pill is an external agent while ability is an internal cause. Following Figure 4, less negative affect should be experienced in the experimental than in the control condition. It is less shameful to fail because of an experimenter-induced drug state than to fail because of low ability. Guided by Expectancy X Value theory, it was hypothesized that subjects low in achievement needs would therefore perform better in the experimental than in the control condition. The pill attribution decreases the aversive consequences (negative incentive value) of failure and thereby increases the motivation to perform the task.

Now consider the subjects high in achievement needs. Their bias to ascribe failure to a lack of effort also is altered by the experimental manipulation and shifts to a drug attribution. The effects of the drug are perceived as stable within the time limit of the experiment, while effort is modifiable. Thus, following Figure 1, the expectancy of future success is lower in the experimental than in the control condition. Effort can be augmented but the detrimental effects of the drug cannot be changed. In addition, the drug is an external agent, while effort expenditure is under personal control. Thus, as discussed already, less negative affect for failure should be experienced in the drug than in the control condition.

In sum, expectancy of success is lower in the pill than in the control condition, but the aversive consequences of failure are lessened by the attribution to the drug. It is therefore difficult to specify the relative *performance* effects of the pill ascription. One of the determinants of behavior

TABLE 5.
The attributional sequence and hypothesized behavior consequences for subjects high and low in achievement needs in the control and experimental (pill) conditions

Achievement Motivation Groups	Low	Low	High	High
Condition	Control	Experimental	Control	Experimental
Failure Attribution	Low Ability	Drug	Low Effort	Drug
Expectancy of Success	Low	Low	High	Low
Negative Affect	High	Low	High	Low
Performance	Low	High	High[1]	Low

[1] Indicates performance relative to same-motive subjects in the alternate condition.

(expectancy) altered by the experimental manipulation functions to *decrease* performance, while the second determinant of behavior (affect) is changed in a direction that should *increase* performance. What is needed to predict the performance effects of the pill attribution is knowledge concerning the relative importance or the weighting of the expectancy versus the affective determinants of behavior.

In a prior paper (Weiner, 1970) I speculated that individuals high in achievement motivation are "realistic" (p. 103). More specifically, it was suggested at that time that individuals highly motivated to succeed weight environmental information and future probabilities of success more heavily than the prior affective consequences of their actions. If this is the case, then the low expectancy of future success in the pill condition would inhibit performance more than the decreased negative affect would enhance achievement strivings. Thus, the performance of individuals high in achievement needs should be lower in the pill than in the control condition. In sum, it was anticipated that the pill attributions relatively would enhance the performance of individuals low in achievement needs, but decrease the performance of persons high in achievement needs.

The combined results of two identical experiments that included 200 subjects are shown in Figure 6. The index of motivation is the improvement in the speed of performance (number of digit substitutions per unit of time) over trials, relative to pre-test performance. Looking first at the results in the control condition, the data indicate that individuals high in achievement needs improve more than subjects low in achievement needs. This result replicates the performance findings in the achievement literature when the motive groups are given failure experiences. On the other hand, in the experimental condition persons low in achievement needs exhibit greater improvement in their speed of performance than subjects in the high motive group.

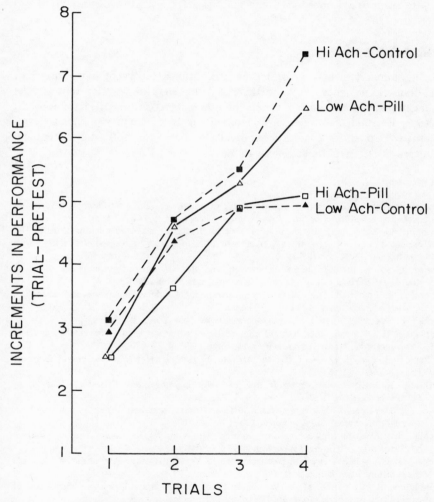

FIG. 6.   Mean increments in performance speed (number of digit-symbol substitutions) relative to pre-test performance on four test trials as a function of the level of achievement needs (high versus low) and the experimental condition (pill versus control). (From Weiner and Sierad, 1974).

Examining the data between experimental conditions but within a motive group reveals that the high achievement-oriented persons do better given their own attributional interpretations (effort ascriptions) than they do in the experimental (drug ascription) condition. Conversely, the subjects low in achievement needs perform with greater intensity in the pill than in the control (ability ascription) condition. These findings are in accord with the hypotheses shown in Table 5.

CONCLUSIONS

In summary, I have presented an attributional theory of motivation that elaborates Expectancy X Value theory. Although causal attributions are the foundations of the model, a variety of other higher processes play important roles as determinants of action. This broad cognitive base may provide a clearer alternative to the mechanistic approaches that have both dominated and hindered the study of human motivation.

REFERENCES

Eswara, H.S. Administration of reward and punishment in relation to ability, effort, and performance. *Journal of Social Psychology*, 1972, *87*, 139-140.
Fontaine, G. Social comparison and some determinants of expected personal control and expected performance in a novel situation. *Journal of Personality and Social Psychology*, 1974, *29* 487-496.
Frieze, I. Studies of information processing and the attributional process. Unpublished doctoral dissertation, University of California, Los Angeles, 1973.
Frieze, I., & Weiner, B. Cue utilization and attributional judgments for success and failure. *Journal of Personality*, 1971, *39*, 591-606.
Heider, F. *The psychology of interpersonal relations.* New York: Wiley, 1958.
Kaplan, R.M., & Swant, S.G. Reward characteristics of appraisal of achievement behavior. *Representative Research in Social Psychology*, 1973, *4*, 11-17.
Kelley, H.H. *Causal schemata and the attribution process.* New York: General Learning Press, 1972.
Kukla, A. Attributional determinants of achievement-related behavior. *Journal of Personality and Social Psychology*, 1972, *21*, 166-174.
Kun, A., & Weiner, B. Necessary versus sufficient causal schemata for success and failure. *Journal of Research in Personality*, 1973, 7, 197-207.
McMahan, I. Relationships between causal attributions and expectancies of success. *Journal of Personality and Social Psychology*, 1973, *28*, 108-114.
Meyer, W.U. Selbstveranwortlichkeit und Leistungsmotivation. Unpublished doctoral dissertation, Ruhr Universität, Bochum, Germany, 1970.
Nierenberg, R., Goldstein, M., & Weiner, B. Preceived causal stability as a determinant of expectancy of success. *Journal of Personality* (in press).
Rest, S., Nierenberg, R., Weiner, B., & Heckhausen, H. Further evidence concerning the effects of perceptions of effort and ability on achievement evaluation. *Journal of Personality and Social Psychology*, 1973, *28*, 187-191.

Rosenbaum, R.M. A dimensional analysis of the perceived causes of success and failure. Unpublished doctoral dissertation, University of California, Los Angeles, 1972.

Rotter, J.B. Generalized expectancies for internal versus external control of reinforcement. *Psychological Monographs*, 1966, *80* (1, Whole No. 609), pp. 1-28.

Tolman, E.C. *Purposive behavior in animals and men*. New York: Appleton-Century-Crofts, 1932.

Weiner, B. New conceptions in the study of achievement motivation. In B.A. Maher (Ed.) *Progress in experimental personality research*. Vol. 5. New York: Academic Press, 1970. pp. 67-109.

Weiner, B. *Theories of motivation: From mechanism to cognition*. Chicago: Rand-McNally, 1972.

Weiner, B., Frieze, I., Kukla, A., Reed, L., Rest, S., & Rosenbaum, R.M. *Perceiving the causes of success and failure*. New York: General Learning Press, 1971.

Weiner, B., Heckhausen, H., Meyer, W.U., & Cook, R.E. Causal ascriptions and achievement motivation: A conceptual analysis of effort and reanalysis of locus of control. *Journal of Personality and Social Psychology*, 1972, *21*, 239-248.

Weiner, B., & Kukla, A. An atributional analysis of achievement motivation. *Journal of Personality and Social Psychology*, 1970, *15*, 1-20.

Weiner, B., Sierad, J. Misattribution for failure and the enhancement of achievement strivings. *Journal of Personality and Social Psychology,* 1974. (in press)

Zander, A., Fuller, R., & Armstrong, W. Attributed pride or shame in group and self. *Journal of Personality and Social Psychology*, 1972, *23*, 346-352.

Cognitive Control of Action

David Birch, John W. Atkinson and Kenneth Bongort

University of Michigan

We, like almost everyone else, believe that cognitive processes have functional significance for behavior. We believe that there is cognitive control of action. Furthermore, we believe that the formulation of a theory that integrates cognitive processes and motivation is of primary importance – even more important at this point in time than new demonstrations of cognitive control of action. We believe that today we badly need the guidance of research that is given only by theory through its systematic approach and clarity of statement.

We conceive of two types of theory that relate cognition to action and opt, at least for now, for one. One type of theory, for which we opt, recognizes that motivational influences on action can differ in source but proposes that the same principles apply to influences from all sources. Thus, action can be instigated and inhibited by influences that originate in the external environment, in the physiology of the individual, and in the individual's cognitive processes; but the functional significance of all three inputs for action is the same. A cognitive theory of motivation of this first type is a portion of a more general, all embracing theory of motivation. We intend to introduce such a theory, in rudimentary form, in this paper.

The second type of cognitive theory of motivation would be one which stated entirely different principles of action for influences arising from cognitive sources as distinct from noncognitive sources. We know of no such theory, but it is interesting to speculate about the characteristics one might have if it existed. We will do a little speculating of that sort later.

Today, in order to be deserving of its label, a theory of motivation of any type must present a systematic and coherent set of principles that makes clear

71

how it is that motivation eventuates in action. And a cognitive theory of motivation must make understandable the motivational significance of cognitive processes for action through such a set of principles. It is not enough for a *theory* of motivation, cognitive or otherwise, merely to point to empirical relationships between certain antecedent events and behavior and to stop there. A theory of motivation must bring order into the domain of motivation and action by integrating into a single system the various measures we take on the streams of thought and action. Thus, a cognitive theory of motivation must do more than merely state that cognition and action are related. It must include principles of action that are coordinated to cognitive events.

The major purpose of this presentation is to illustrate how the principles that constitute our general theory of motivation, a theory we call the dynamics of action, can be coordinated to cognitive events. In this way, we outline the beginnings of a cognitive theory of motivation of the first type. Our hypothesis is that the conscious products of cognitive processes have motivational implications for action — that they participate in the control of action — and that they have these implications according to the general principles of motivation already set out in the dynamics of action. We will begin by reminding you of some of the fundamental features of the dynamics of action (Atkinson and Birch, 1970).

TABLE 1.
Two paradigms for the study of motivation

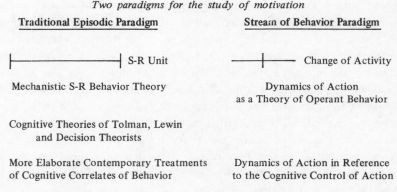

Traditional Episodic Paradigm	Stream of Behavior Paradigm
├──────────────┤ S-R Unit	───────┼─────── Change of Activity
Mechanistic S-R Behavior Theory	Dynamics of Action as a Theory of Operant Behavior
Cognitive Theories of Tolman, Lewin and Decision Theorists	
More Elaborate Contemporary Treatments of Cognitive Correlates of Behavior	Dynamics of Action in Reference to the Cognitive Control of Action

In the dynamics of action we break with tradition and abandon the conventional S-O-R paradigm of psychology. Table 1 draws attention to several of the important differences between the new and old paradigms. The old paradigm, anchored ultimately in Descartes' idea of reflex and the concept of a stimulus-bound brain, served as the setting for the classic debate between Guthrie, Tolman, and Hull in the 30's and 40's. Within the S-O-R paradigm, behavioral life is implicitly viewed as a series of goal-directed episodes. Each of these units of study is marked off at the beginning by the occurrence of a stimulus and at the end by the occurrence of a response. Several quantifiable questions have been asked about these episodes – willingness to initiate an action (latency), selection among alternative means to a goal (choice), vigor of action, and persistence of a goal-directed pursuit.

The new paradigm takes a different view of behavioral life. This results in a redefinition of the problem of motivation and a reconstruction of the theory of motivation. Instead of viewing behavioral life as a sequence of S-O-R episodes, the new paradigm begins with the premise of an ever-active organism whose behavioral life is a stream of activity characterized by change from one activity to another. Within this new paradigm, the problem of motivation becomes, initially, that of analyzing changes of activity.

Interestingly enough, the conceptual analysis of a single change from one activity to another, the most fundamental problem of motivation within the new paradigm, has brought new order into the domain defined by the traditional episodic paradigm. For example, the initiation of activity and the persistence of activity are treated as separate problems in the episodic paradigm but turn out to be only different aspects of the same problem in the new paradigm. In our analysis, it soon became apparent that a single event, a change from one activity to another, and the clock reading for that event defined both the persistence of the initially ongoing activity and the latency of initiation of the new activity. Furthermore, we discovered that choice, another of the classic problems in the episodic paradigm, is implicit in any change of activity. As a consequence, it was possible to establish a coherent, integrative thread that ties together the several traditional episodic measures of the behavioral expression of motivation by deriving a simple principle of change of activity.

Figure 1 shows in schematic form the five ways in which a change from one activity to another can occur theoretically. We begin our analysis of motivation by proposing that at any moment in time the ongoing activity expresses the strongest tendency to action. Thus, to say that activity A is ongoing initially is also to say that the tendency to engage in activity A is stronger than the tendency to engage in activity B (or any other activity) initially. This is the case in each of the five graphs in Figure 1. Furthermore, to say that activity changes from A to B is also to say that the tendency to engage in activity B has come to dominate the tendency to engage in activity A. The five patterns by which this change in the dominance relations between tendencies can occur over time is also shown.

By introducing some notation and making use of a little algebra, we can derive a statement concerning the time it takes for a change of activity under these simple conditions. If we let T_{A_I} and T_{B_I} be the initial strengths of tendencies for activities A and B and T_{A_F} and T_{B_F} be their final strengths (i.e., their strengths at the time the change of activity occurs), we can derive the

73

equation: $t_{B/A} = \left(T_{A_F} - T_{B_I}\right)/F_B$. In this equation, $t_{B/A}$ is the time required for the change of activity. It is easily seen to be both the latency of activity B and the persistence of activity A. And F_B is the average rate of change in the strength of the tendency for activity B. We call F_B the *instigating force* for activity B.

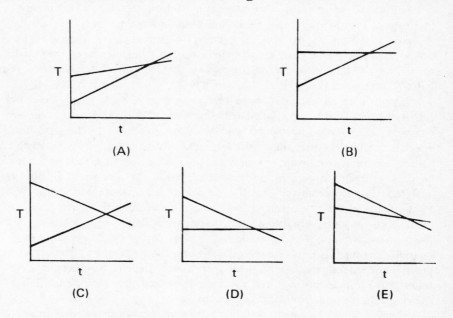

FIG. 1. *Schematic representation of the five types of change of activity.*

Figure 2 illustrates how the analysis of a change of activity leads automatically to an analysis of choice. In the graph on the left, X is chosen over Y because the tendency for X, rather than the tendency for Y, dominates the tendency for the initially ongoing choice point activity. Note that this occurred even though the tendency for Y is initially stronger than the tendency for X. In the graph on the right, the very special case is shown in which the tendencies for X and Y reach the level of the tendency for the choice point activity simultaneously. This condition is important theoretically because it specifies a pivotal set of relationships such that any deviation in any parameter value for any tendency will determine the choice of either X or Y. Proceeding in this way, we found it possible to state mathematically the relative frequencies of choices for certain special conditions and in this fashion reduced the problem of choice to that of a change of activity.

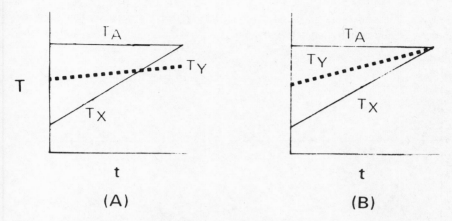

FIG. 2. Two examples of a simple choice between alternatives X and Y according to the dynamics of action.

When the analysis is extended to the constantly changing stream of activity in a constant, unchanging environment, the principle of change of activity embraces the measures of time spent in given activities, the relative frequency of occurrence of activities, and the derivative measure of rate or operant level of particular activities. It is appropriate to say that this theoretical development constitutes a theory of operant behavior (Birch, 1972).

Figure 3 depicts the theoretical correspondence between the stream of activity, shown in the segmented line at the top, and the ever-changing strengths of corresponding tendencies pictured below. Each of the letters X, Y, and Z stands for an activity. The operant behavior of the individual over the interval presented is generated by the interplay among the tendencies for those activities, as shown in the lower portion of the figure.

The theory of motivation as reconstructed in *The Dynamics of Action* begins by noting that a change in activity can occur only if the relative strength of the inclinations, or motivational tendencies, of an individual change. It goes on to identify the causal factors responsible for these changes in motivation and how they operate over time.

Certain of these factors are to be found in the immediate environment of an individual[1], which is seen as providing psychological forces on an individual to engage or not to engage in various activities. The prior life experience of the individual determines what forces, with what magnitudes, are imposed by the environment. If a certain kind of activity has been intrinsically satisfying or rewarded in this kind of situation, there will be an *instigating force* for that

---

[1] The locus of the discriminative stimuli in the literature on operant behavior.

activity. This will cause an increase in the strength of the person's tendency to undertake that activity, an *action tendency*.

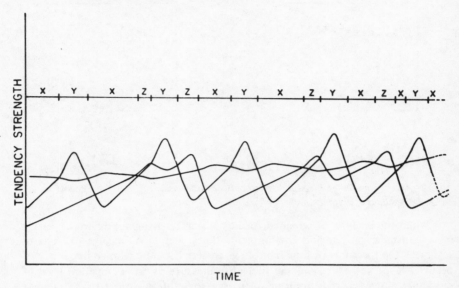

FIG. 3. *An example of a stream of activity and its underlying tendency structure.*

As pictured in Figure 4, the increase in the strength of an action tendency can be continuous or not depending on whether or not the individual is exposed continuously to the instigating force. The central point, however, is that exposure to an instigating force increases the strength of a tendency over the duration of that exposure.

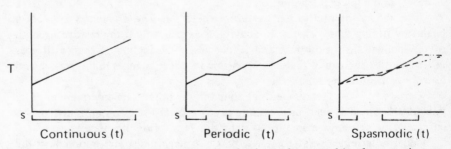

FIG. 4. *Examples of the growth in the strength of a tendency resulting from continuous and noncontinuous exposure to an instigating force.*

If a certain kind of activity has been punished or frustrated in the past, the environment will be the source of an *inhibitory force* and there will be growth in the strength of *negaction tendency*, i.e., a tendency *not* to engage in that

76

activity. The anticipation of a negative consequence for engaging in an activity, which has the functional significance of an inhibitory force acting to increase the strength of a negaction tendency, produces *resistance* to engaging in an activity. A negaction tendency opposes an action tendency and dampens the resultant strength of the inclination to act.

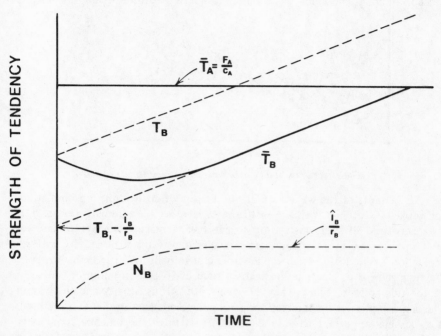

FIG. 5. *Illustration of the delay in initiating an activity because of the presence of resistance to that activity.*

Figure 5 shows how the presence of resistance to an activity delays the initiation of that activity. Note how the growth of the negaction tendency for activity B subtracts from the action tendency for activity B to produce a resultant action tendency that takes longer to reach the level of tendency for activity A than would have been the case had no negaction been present. Note also that a stronger, compensating action tendency that has been produced during the extra time required for the change of activity. This phenomenon of "bottling up" action tendencies has several important implications for the stream of behavior that we are just beginning to appreciate.

The *resultant action tendency*, defined as the strength of the action tendency minus the strength of the negaction tendency, competes with the resultant action tendencies to engage in other activities. The strongest is

77

expressed in the observable stream of behavior. The expression of a motivational tendency in behavior constitutes a *consummatory force* which acts to reduce the strength of that tendency. In parallel fashion, resistance to an action tendency by a negaction tendency is sufficient to produce a *force of resistance* which acts to reduce the strength of the negaction tendency. This, in brief, presents our conception about the main causal factors responsible for the stream of behavior.

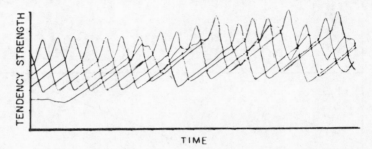

FIG. 6. *The effect of resistance to one activity on the stream of activity.*

An example of the way in which the factors of instigation, consummation, and resistance interact is shown in Figure 6. Here we have initially a context of four activities all with instigating forces having magnitudes of 16, and no inhibitory forces. In addition, there is a tendency for a fifth activity with no instigation or inhibition from the environment initially. A little later, however, the environment produces an instigating force of 16 and an inhibitory force of 32 for this activity. The latency of occurrence of this activity and the way in which it complicates the interactions among the tendencies in the set is pictured. It is perhaps important to note, particularly at this time, that the complexity results from the dynamic processes set forth in the theory and not from an appeal to a constantly changing environment. The environment changes once in Figure 6, but the complexities follow from the new and constant conditions, not from the change itself.

Since 1970, when the *Dynamics of Action* was published, Robert Seltzer has written a computer program for the theory (Seltzer, 1973). It is Seltzer's program which generated and plotted the theoretical curves presented so far. The program, developed further with James Sawusch (Seltzer and Sawusch, 1974), is now available in the appendix of a new book, *Motivation and Achievement*, edited by Atkinson and Raynor (1974). Having this program available has been an immense help to us in arriving at expectations from the theory because the mathematical statements themselves quickly become unmanageable when several activities are considered in the stream. This level of complexity is the one that needs to be dealt with theoretically, however, if we are to face up to the basic problems in the domain of motivation.

An example of one of the earliest products from our computer program has already been presented in Figure 3. This graph was drawn by the computer illustrating what the stream of behavior might be if an individual were exposed to instigating forces of different magnitudes for three incompatible activities in a *constant* environment, i.e., an environment in which no changes in any instigating or inhibitory forces occurred. The path of each tendency is determined completely by the fixed set of parameter values operating in conjunction with the theory. The stream of behavior is given by the sequence of dominant tendencies across the time interval.

Both Figures 3 and 6 show clearly that there can be inclinations to act in certain ways, within an individual, that carry over from the past and are quite independent of the present stimulus situation. In fact, the strengths of tendencies for all activities at any point in time are determined by the operation of the forces (instigating, consummatory, inhibitory, and resistance) on the strengths of tendencies present at the just previous point in time.

In our earliest considerations of the stream of behavior, as illustrated in Figure 3, we paid little formal attention to the origin of forces. We tended to think only of the external environment as the source of instigating and inhibitory forces because that was simplest in our efforts to understand the dynamics of the theory. As we have gained that understanding, we have begun to ask how forces originating in the cognitive processes of an individual might relate to action.

In the *Dynamics of Action*, we take only a first few tentative steps in accommodating thought to action. For example, in Chapter 6 entitled "Cognitive Correlates" we show how the cognitive theory of achievement motivation can be coordinated with the concepts of instigating and inhibitory forces. This coordination serves the very important purpose of opening up the theoretical resources of the dynamics of action to the achievement domain.

The coordination of the cognitive theory of achievement motivation, which employs the concepts of expectancy and valence, with the dynamics of action represents one of the ways in which cognitive control of action can be conceptualized. The cognitive processes of the individual operating on inputs from the environment determine the values of instigating and inhibitory forces which, in turn, determine the stream of behavior. The important point here is that two theories, one of cognition and the other of motivation, are joined, making an overall theory of cognitive control of action. Recently, the early cognitive theory of achievement motivation has been elaborated by Joel Raynor (1969, 1974) and his co-workers so as to include the motivational impact on some immediate activity of a contingent path from that activity to more distant gains and losses. This advance in cognitive theory is also easily coordinated with the principles of the dynamics of action and appears in this form in Atkinson and Raynor (1974).

The coordination of cognitive theory with motivation theory is important in understanding how cognition controls action, but we think cognitive processes also have a more direct functional significance for action. We think that conscious thought can be a source of instigating and inhibitory forces. We propose that the thought of eating steak, i.e., the *content* of that thought, instigates the action tendency for the overt activity of seeking steak to eat. We also propose that the content of every thought can instigate and inhibit the covert activity of thinking that thought. In general, then, we propose that the contents of conscious thought constitute a source of instigating and inhibitory forces both for the covert activity of thinking that thought and for the overt activity referenced by that thought.

This proposal further frees the individual from the control of the immediate stimulus environment. The individual was first freed from immediate environmental control in the dynamics of action by allowing an action tendency to arise in one setting and to persist to find expression in another setting where instigation for that activity was completely lacking. Now, in addition, the *products* of an individual's cognitive processes can enter equally with the environment as inputs to the total configuration of forces operative at any particular moment in time.

Historically, this elaboration of the theory grows out of the second of three possibilities concerning the relation of the content of thought and action outlined in the final chapter of the *Dynamics of Action*. The possibilities set forth there were as follows: (1) The content of thought and action run parallel and are often correlated because they have a common origin in the past history of the individual, but they do not control each other; (2) Actions can be instigated and/or resisted without anything in the content of conscious thought being diagnostic of these processes, but actions can also be instigated and/or resisted by the contents of conscious thought; and (3) All instigation to action and resistance to action *must* be mediated by conscious thought. An implication of the second view is that the thought of engaging in some activity would *amplify* a process already implicit in the conditions of the moment which had instigated both the inclination to think about that activity and the correlated inclination to undertake the activity.

This latter view of the relation of the content of thought to action is the one adopted for the illustration of cognitive control of action we wish to present today. We have chosen what we think to be a fairly dramatic example of cognitive control of action and use the principles from the dynamics of action to show how we think it might occur.

Consider the following scenario: We arrive in the middle of the morning one day to discover a professor alone in his house busily engaged in riding his exercise bicycle. He is in the basement, which is well insulated from all outside stimulation — auditory, olfactory, and visual. In the room, in addition to the

80

bicycle, are some old publications about baseball and his briefcase sitting near the door. Let's assume that the room is empty otherwise and that the only sound comes from the professor's efforts to move the immovable bicycle. As we watch, no overt activity other than bicycle riding occurs until suddenly the professor stops pedaling, gets off the bicycle, and goes upstairs and writes a letter to his brother.

What we have observed is the spontaneous initiation of letter writing in an environment which contains no stimulus in any way related to letter writing. The basement room provides instigating forces for the overt activities of bicycle riding, working, and going to the library for a book about the old New York Giants. It also provides instigation for the covert activities of *thinking* about bicycle riding, *thinking* about working, and *thinking* about going to the library for a book about the old New York Giants. We assume that nowhere in the environment is there instigation to write letters or to think about writing letters. Yet our subject is observed to change, apparently spontaneously, from the overt activity of bicycle riding to the overt activity of writing a letter to his brother.

Using the dynamics of action as the theoretical tool, our analysis of such a spontaneous change of activity suggests that what we have observed is a fairly dramatic and pure example of a way in which cognition can control action. Figure 7 depicts the essential elements of this analysis.[2]

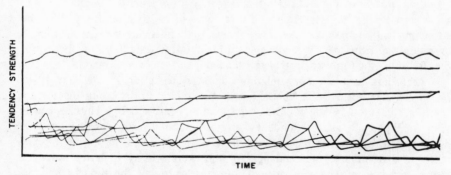

FIG. 7. *An example of the cognitive control of action simulated from the dynamics of action.*

Note first the separate streams of overt activity and thought. To keep things simple we will assume that engaging in each overt activity (bicycle riding, working, going to the library or writing a letter) is incompatible with engaging in every other overt activity. We shall also assume that there can be only one

---

[2] Kenneth Bongort has recently improved and extended the capacity of our computer program during his term as a predoctoral fellow of the National Science Foundation.

thought in consciousness at a time. This means that the *thoughts* of riding, working, going to the library, and letter writing are mutually incompatible. Finally, we shall assume complete compatibility between thinking any thought and engaging in any overt activity.

In Figure 7, note that only the overt activity of bicycle riding is ongoing throughout the interval of observation until the very end when the professor heads upstairs to write the letter. During this interval, however, there occurs a stream of covert activities involving all four thoughts.

Thinking about letter writing occurs in this situation for two reasons. First, there is present an inertial tendency to think about writing a letter derived out of the professor's earlier exposures to stimuli with the capacity to instigate such thoughts. In particular, the professor may have walked past a table on his way to the basement on which a recently received letter from his brother was lying or engaged in a conversation about his brother at breakfast. These events could be expected to increase his tendency to think about writing a letter to his brother.

The second reason that thinking about letter writing occurs in this environment, which contains no instigation to do so, is that there is no strong instigation to think about anything else, either. The professor arrived in the basement preoccupied with thinking about bicycle riding (i.e., with a strong tendency to think about bicycle riding) and the instigation from the basement room was not sufficient to sustain this tendency. Consequently, the tendency to think about bicycle riding falls and gives way to another tendency. With no strong instigation present in the environment, the tendencies decrease in strength over time until the inertial tendency to think about writing to his brother is, for the first time, the professor's strongest tendency in the covert domain.

According to the theory relating cognition to action that we favor, the functional significance of a thought is that its *content* provides instigation for thinking that thought and for the corresponding overt activity. Thus, as can be seen in Figure 7, as the tendency to think about letter writing becomes dominant in the covert stream it rises to its asymptote and, during the interval when it is dominant, the tendency for the overt activity of letter writing is strengthened. The same property of joint instigation of the thought and the action can be observed for the other thoughts and actions. They are, however, also instigated from the environment, in contrast to letter writing and thinking about letter writing. That is why the tendencies related to working and going to the library and to thinking about working and thinking about going to the library rise the way they do during these intervals, but the tendencies related to letter writing and thinking about letter writing do not. As time passes and the stream of thought continues there is a gradual strengthening of the professor's tendency to write a letter to his brother, until at some point the tendency to write dominates the tendency to ride the bicycle and there is a change of activity.

What has been outlined in this scenario is truly an example of the cognitive control of action. The genesis of the overt activity of writing a letter is solely in the spontaneous thoughts of the individual, with absolutely no support from the immediate external environment.

This analysis of an instance of cognitive control of action derives out of the dynamics of action in a very straightforward fashion. No new principles of motivation need be entertained. All that need be done is to allow instigation and inhibition (though the latter was not a factor in our example) to originate in the content of thought as well as in the external environment. With a theory of motivation already at hand, a *cognitive* theory of motivation is easily attained by coordinating the functional significance of cognitions to the dynamics of action.

As we mentioned at the beginning of the paper, however, it is possible to conceive of another type of theory that relates cognition to action. A theory of this other type would propose entirely different principles of action. According to the dynamics of action, tendencies are responsible for action and tendencies gain strength continuously over time as a consequence of duration of exposure to instigation. The same principles are proposed to hold for thoughts — a thought is in consciousness when the tendency for that thought is dominant and tendencies for thoughts are strengthened by instigation over time. The key principle to be noted is that the tendencies change in strength gradually as a function of the duration of exposure to instigation.

One might propose additional or alternative principles and thereby provide the basis for a different cognitive theory of motivation. For example, we think it conceivable that thoughts might come into consciousness via principles other than exposure to instigation. Here we have in mind such phenomena as insight, inference, and deduction. There appear to be cognitive processes which are not governed by principles of exposure to instigation but which, nevertheless, have as their outcome the emergence of a thought into consciousness. Thus, we anticipate that additional principles beyond exposure to instigation will be required in order to deal comprehensively with the stream of thought.

One could, of course, add to the number of principles governing the stream of thought and still hold to a single duration of exposure principle relating thought to action. That is, one could propose theoretically that a thought can come into consciousness in more than one way but, given that this happens, it matters not how it happens. It only matters that the content of the thought functions as a force to change the strength of a tendency during the interval of time it is present.

On the other hand, we can also conceive of alternative principles by which thought and action are related. For example, perhaps some actions are the direct result of a cognitive process. It may be that when we generate the verbal command to ourselves, "I must write a letter to my brother right now," that we write the letter as a direct result of the command, if the command is compelling enough. Perhaps action is derived from thought in a discontinuous, direct fashion on some occasions. We can see how this might be the case even though we don't see what the principles are.

In this presentation we have extended the implications of the principle of exposure to instigation and inhibition over time as developed in the dynamics of action to cover a particular type of relationship between cognition and action. At the same time, we can conceive of other kinds of relationships calling for different principles. What is essential for any cognitive theory of motivation, we emphasize, is that it contain explicit statements of how action is determined by cognition and that these statements be used to derive expected characterisitcs of the measureable stream of behavior.

The rebirth of interest in cognitive approaches to motivation must not lead to theories which — in a paraphrase of Guthrie's quip about Tolman's rats — leave the individual lost in thought. Nor can we be satisfied with the very limited conception of the behavioral problem of motivation in the traditional episodic paradigm. We are well past the point of taking much satisfaction in mere correlations between something cognitive and some behavioral index. The new cognitive approach to motivation must be as new and as contemporary in its understanding of problems of motivation as it aspires to be in its treatment of cognition.

REFERENCES

Atkinson, J.W., & Birch, D. *The dynamics of action*. New York-London: John Wiley and Sons, 1970.

Atkinson, J.W., & Raynor, J.O. (Eds.) *Motivation and achievement*. Washington, D.C.: V.H. Winston, (Distributed by Halsted Press of John Wiley & Co.), 1974.

Birch, D. Measuring the stream of activity. Michigan Mathematical Psychology Program, 1972.

Raynor, J.O. Future orientations and motivation of immediate activity: An elaboration of the theory of achievement motivation. *Psychological Review*, 1969, *76*, 606-610. Reprinted with experiments and elaborations in Atkinson, J.W. and Raynor, J.O. (Eds.) *Motivation and achievement*. Washington, D.C.: V.H. Winston (Distributed by Halsted Press of John Wiley & Co.), 1974.

Seltzer, R.A. Simulation of the dynamics of action. *Psychological Reports*, 1973, *32* 859-872.

Seltzer, R.A., & Sawusch, J.R. A program for computer simulation of the dynamics of action. In Atkinson, J.W. and Raynor, J.O. (Eds.) *Motivation and achievement*. Washington, D.C.: V.H. Winston (Distributed by Halsted Press of John Wiley & Co.), 1974.

Discussion

Robert R. Sears

Stanford University

Bolles' historical introduction gives an excellent backdrop against which to view the four research papers. They give four quite different accounts of the way in which cognitive processes enter into the expression of motivation in behavior. Three of them are mini-theories which describe, with research support, some of the cognitive variables that are relevant to particular behavioral outcomes. The fourth, that of Birch, Atkinson, and Bongort, is more a macro-theory which depends less upon precise research predictions than on its internal coherence as a way of talking about motivation and behavioral outcomes. So, now it is proper to ask what have these new uses of cognition given us that we did not have before?

Cognition has become a fashionable term in the past few years. Indeed, it is so very fashionable, and has been used in so many ways by so many people, that it no longer has a single technical meaning. Like the words motivation and personality, it has become a textbook chapter heading. The meaning given it by Mischel, however, seems pretty well to cover the ways in which the present authors use it. Mischel referred to processes that go on *inside the black box*. These belong to the realms of perception, thinking and reasoning, remembering and recalling, and all the many mental manipulations that make use of such functions. The manipulations include planning and coping, and unconscious as well as conscious processes. The black box is a metaphorical reference to one part of the 'O' – the organism in Woodworth's old formulation of S-O-R. The input hits the organism, is transformed by all the many mental operations, and finally behavior comes out. I agree with Bolles that Woodworth made a step away from sheer mechanism, and also that it was only a step. It did not include much emphasis on the active, internal instigation to action. Nevertheless, Woodworth's -O- was the precursor to our contemporary references to the black box.

85

From a logical and theoretical standpoint, the transformational processes that go on in the box are essentially no more than intervening variables between input and output. As Mischel has emphasized, they can be of value to the extent that their nature can be precisely defined in terms of operations *external* to the black box, operations that can be observed or controlled by empirical means. Unfortunately, not all intervening variables have always met this criterion, and in recent years there has been some tendency for those most rigorous theoreticians (who are more devoted to parsimony than to reality) to disavow intervening variables altogether. Actually, every theory of human motivation has been cognitive in one way or another. Today's self-conscious emphasis on the cognitive element provides nothing very novel, from a theoretical standpoint, but it is certainly a welcome change from the sterility of pigeon-brain behaviorism. For much too long we have been subjected to alleged theory and self-proclaimed non-theory by psychologists who seem pathologically afraid of the dark — that is, the darkness in the black box. It is a relief to hear again some theoretical formulations that *do* explore the hypothetical events going on there.

Historically, the great motivational theories have always depended heavily on cognitive processes. Psychoanalytic theory is pre-eminent in this respect, with its emphasis on the ego and the defense mechanisms. McDougall's theory of instincts — in tune with the *fin de siecle* emphasis on pre-programmed behavior patterns — accounted for behavioral outcomes as a product of very complex, built-in cognitive processes. In 1918, Woodworth's dynamic psychology offered a similar account, but with learning taking the place of instinctual programming. Only in recent years has the black box ostensibly disappeared from behavior theory. But even pigeon-brain behaviorism invokes such principles as reinforcement, extinction, inhibition, shaping, and fading to account for regularities in behavioral output from stimulus input. Even this spare non-theory implies internal mechanisms of transformation and storage.

So, I think there is no such thing as a cognitive *theory* of motivation, and a cognitive *view* means simply that we are looking at the cognitive aspects of the total motivational process. All the present views have their roots in historical efforts to solve the same theoretical problems. The Birch-Atkinson-Bongort system is easily identified as the 35-year-old formulation presented in *Frustration and Aggression*, which in turn stemmed from a reworking of Freud, McDougall, G.V. Hamilton, Woodworth and others. Cognition enters when they discover that conscious thought or remembered plans can influence behavior. I confess this seems less dramatic to me than it does to them. Certainly neither Hull nor Tolman would have been astonished either by that observation or by the notion that the stream of behavior involves a constant interweaving of activities having varied antecedents, varied purposes, and varied outcomes in relation to varied goal objects. Both Hull and Tolman saw purposive behavior as a major phenomenon requiring explanation, and both recognized the constant existence of conflicts among simultaneously instigated responses, with shifting dominances producing alternating action patterns.

One matter troubles me with respect to the Birch-Atkinson-Bongort presentation. How a computer program helps in an understanding of this latter process is not clear to me. A computer can be of use in simulating input-output relationships only when quantitative constants and variables can be introduced into the program. That is what would be needed to permit effective use of such a program. It seems to me that the Birch-Atkinson-Bongort formulation provides a kind of heuristic abstraction which is convenient for describing a behavioral sequence, but it is not properly a theory about empirical data, either experimental or naturalistic. So far, the cognitive element seems to be defined as *conscious thought*, with no operational definitions either of that concept itself or of the many mental transformations it seems to subsume.

Weiner's formulation is much more closely attached to experimentally obtained data. It stems from two major sources, Lewin's field theory and person-perception theory. I include in the former Lewin's empirical adjuncts of level of aspiration, frustration, and reward and punishment principles. In part, Weiner's theory offers a set of response-response rather than stimulus-response principles. In this respect, it is different from the other three formulations presented here. For example, one variable – a child's judgment of task difficulty – is related to another – the outcome of how hard he works on it. The former is measured by the subject's verbal behavior and the latter by the quality of his performance on the task itself. Were Weiner's propositions to stop here, we would be justified in raising a skeptical eyebrow as to their value, for while response-response correlations are necessary for the study of personality or motivational structure, they are of limited use in a theory of action. He has not fallen into that trap, however, and he has been particularly ingenious in following the principle that there must be operational definitions for the conditions under which particular perceptions are created. It is in this area of external conditions of control of cognitive variables that Weiner's formulation becomes ultimately a stimulus-response theory. What makes it cognitive, however, is the precise way in which he has defined what goes on in the black box. What goes on, of course, is the set of perceptions that the child has with respect to the four major variables that Weiner has defined as being relevant both to the child's achievement performance and to his feelings about his performance.

Mischel's formulation stems from a long line of learning and action theorists whose latest flag still flies, after a third of a century, with the label of social learning theory that was applied to the tradition by Miller and Dollard. Mischel has chosen action theory rather than learning theory as his field for work since delay of gratification (an action) is the dependent variable or behavioral outcome for which he has sought antecedents. Unlike Weiner, Mischel makes no interpretations about the black box processes that involve the subject's own perceptions. He defines intervening variables, such as attention, imagery, and reality perceptions, in terms of the operational conditions that give rise to them. These hypothetical states are just as cognitive and just as much a part of the black box operation as are those of Weiner, which *sound* more cognitive because they are more explicitly described in terms of the person's perception. The beautiful precision of Mischel's successive experimental interventions has enabled him to discover the nature of the cognitive processes which influence the child's capacity of delaying gratification. When I say the *nature* of the processes, I do not go beyond his own strictures. The processes are not defined by the conscious or reportable qualities of the perceptions, but by the conditions that create them. They may be hypothetical constructs and they may operate as intervening variables, but they are rooted in operational defintions. Although Mischel is in the tradition of pure stimulus-response theorists, he is far from being tainted with the sterility of operant conditioning principles or pure S-R theoretical structures. The latter may have value for simple psychological engineering, as with learning machines or behavior modification therapies, but Mischel has wisely chosen to stick with reality when he works on such a complex process as delay of gratification.

Now consider Lazarus' formulation. He has concerned himself primarily with the coping process. This is a broad enough problem, in all conscience, and the dependent variables with which he works are much more complex than those to which Weiner and Mischel have devoted themselves. They are less clearly defined than are theirs. *Coping* itself – the intervening variables that refer to what goes on in the black box – is the substance of his study, and the operations that define it are multiple rather than singular. Mischel has a standard measure of gratification delay and Weiner has measures of achievement performance and reported feelings. Lazarus, however, uses anything that comes to hand which can serve as a measured outcome. He has used endocrine measures as well as reported feelings and overt behavior. His antecedents range from examination failure in adolescents to critical surgery in adults, and even to parents' having to face a fatal illness in a child. For Lazarus, the black box is much more like Woodworth's total organism – O – than it is for the other theorists. It contains the cognitive elements to which they have pointed, to be sure, but it contains a great deal more, what might reasonably be called the total response potential of the person. If this complexity has forced him to use less neat and precise antecedents and consequences than Weiner and Mischel have been able to devise, we can hardly complain. Like them, he is concerned to discover what goes on inside the black box – not just to play a zero-sum game of non-theory.

So much for the individual contributions. In the mass, what do they tell us? First, they bring cognitive processes back into the limelight, so far as motivation and personality behaviors are concerned. The black box cannot be ignored.

There are regularities in the transformation processes that extend far beyond the simplistic relations between sensory input and behavioral output that have been so widely exploited by pigeon-brain behaviorism. Whatever value the latter may have for psychological engineering, it clearly can be improved upon by giving attention to the transformation processes which – in man as contrasted with pigeons – provide for enormous behavioral variation in the behavioral outcomes of motivation.

Second, however, I must take a more provocative and demanding position. The precision of three of the four research programs is splendid, but their breadth is limited. I would like to see an extension of both Weiner's and Mischel's analyses to some dependent variables other than achievement behavior and delay of gratification. Mini-theories are useful and I have the greatest admiration for both of these, but they must be extended to more than a single dependent variable. I would like to see Lazarus do just the opposite and bring his data on coping into a somewhat more precise theoretical structure. So far, his data deal mainly with anxiety and frustration as motives, but, unlike the psychoanalysts, he has had the courage to talk about coping in relation to pleasurable motives, too. What I want, believe it or not, is less empirics and more hard propositionalizing. As to the Birch-Atkinson-Bongort formulation, I look forward to seeing some concrete data that will warrant the use of both their heuristic scheme and their computer program.

Third, and finally, I must return to my initial comment about the history of motivation. As Bolles has said, there is nothing new about the cognitive element. It was an important part of Freud's and McDougall's theories. It entered as an explicit part of G.V. Hamilton's primate research and his theory and therapeutic practice with human patients. It was inherent in Woodworth's dynamic psychology half a century ago, and it was an essential aspect of the purposive behavior emphasis in the theoretical analyses of both Hull and Tolman.

What Bolles did not discuss sufficiently, perhaps, was the continuing trend from the mid-30s toward the use of black box concepts in theories of human motivation. Both Hull and Tolman were fundamentally rat psychologists and their conceptions of motivation were severely limited. By using them as mainstream models in the history of motivation, Bolles limits his history to the narrow field of animal motivation theory. Even Lewin's rich and exciting field theory is reduced to a kind of Tolmanian sub-species. If one were to expand the history to cover the more important field of human motivation, there are several additional steps that would need describing. These are less rigorously traditional in allegiance to experimental psychology, but they are more revealing of the exact point to which Bolles' animal motivation history leads us – namely, the increasing dependence on cognitive processes as a part of motivation.

One would need to include the fairly elaborate conceptions of personality, with much attention to "needs," that were developed among child guidance clinicians in the 1920s. Such concepts as love, rejection, sibling rivalry, and aspiration are all motivational concepts. The complex system of needs and presses constructed by Murray deserves recognition, and so does the "autonomous motive" of Gordon Allport. Likewise, the concept of acquired drive as developed by Miller and Dollard was an important step in the development of motivation theory. Its application in my own research and theory construction in the field of child rearing and personality development was not irrelevant, for it served not only as the focus for an extensive research movement but as a rejectable theoretical base from which the newer and more effective theory of motivation in the work of Bandura, Walters, and Mischel arose. And certainly a history of human motivation theory is incomplete without reference to the essentially dyadic theory of attachment of Bowlby, with its precursors in the British psychoanalytic theories of Melanie Klein and Anna Freud, and the primate work of Harlow. In every instance, the cognitive element in human motivation theory — that is, the use of explanatory concepts referring to the hypothetical contents of the black box — has been strong and central. So I can agree fully with Bolles' conclusions that Mechanism did not work. I cannot forebear to point out that no psychologist of *human* motivation ever bothered to try it!

Cognition really is not a novelty. What *is* new in recent years, and what is so well displayed by the present contributions, is the shift from clinical data to more precisely controlled experimental and naturalistic data. Motivation cannot be understood in terms of drive alone, nor in terms of cognitive transformations alone. It is not a product of just the environment nor of just the organism. It is not the product of just nature nor of just nurture. A thousand years from now, when motivation is finally fully understood, all these parameters will be taken into account. In the meantime, good hard data — experimental, clinical, naturalistic — well mixed with good hard theory — both mini and macro — will be solid steps along the way.

Comments on the Discussion

David Birch and John W. Atkinson

University of Michigan

It is a disappointment to find that for Professor Sears the dynamics of action is "easily identified as the 35-year-old formulation presented in *Frustration and Agression*." We had hoped that the discontinuity between our dynamics of action and the behavior theories of the past would be as obvious as some of the continuities to which he alludes. The difference between the old and the new is the difference between recognizing *that* motivational processes exist and specifying *how* those processes proceed through time. Cognition did not enter the dynamics of action when we discovered *that* conscious thought or remembered plans can influence behavior, as Professor Sears suggests, but rather cognition entered when we discovered a way to specify *how* they might do so.

Not unexpectedly, it turns out that specifying motivational processes, with or without cognition included, results in a complex system for any situation beyond the very simplest ones. The analysis of the stream of activity is a complex business and we have therefore turned to the computer for assistance. The computer helps us to understand the stream of activity by its capacity to come up with the implications of simple principles applied to complex antecedent conditions. The computer program *is* the theory. Its use contributes to the understanding of behavior to the extent that the dynamics of action contributes.

When applied to data, the dynamics of action has been helpful in understanding a number of well-known empirical generalizations about the behavioral effects of reward training and punishment training (Atkinson & Birch, 1970) and certain phenomena of food deprivation in rats (Birch, 1968). This theoretical scheme has been used to provide a coherent account of how measured motivational differences in personality (viz., need for achievement and test anxiety) are expressed in action (see Atkinson & Birch, 1970, 1974). The result, we think, is a theory of achievement-oriented activity which achieves a goal that Sears (1951) himself set for the study of personality many years ago: to describe the individual in terms of potentialities for action for which there are known principles.

Professor Weiner, in his contribution to this symposium, directs our attention to a different aspect of the study of achievement motivation. He emphasizes the need to broaden our conception of the cognitive antecedents of the motivational variables (viz., expectancy and value) that have proven useful in the integration of facts concerning achievement-related activities. We agree. This is important. Yet sometimes we think that those most committed to the new cognitive approach (see also Heckhausen, 1973) tend to underestimate the power of some very simple ideas that have already been advanced concerning antecedents of subjective probability of success. We have in mind the paper by Jones, *et al.* (1968) and the cognitive elaboration of the theory of achievement motivation by Raynor (1969, 1974). The latter effectively captures the impact on action of distant future goals and threats. The attributional approach, as presented by Weiner, is clearly meant to complement, not to replace, conceptions like the elaborated expectancy-value theory or the new dynamics of action.

In relating the new cognitive approach to achievement motivation to already existing theory, it is informative to make use of the last experiment Weiner reports. In this experiment the behavior of subjects who are told that a placebo drug they are given will interfere with performance of a task is compared to that of a comparable group of subjects who are given a typical Achievement Orientation. This comparison appears very much the same as that made by Atkinson (1953) in an early examination of the effects on the Zeigarnik effect of Relaxed Orientation versus Achievement Orientation among individuals who differ in *n* Achievement. Then it was stated: "The different instructions were designed to vary the probability that Ss would perceive completion of tasks as evidence of personal accomplishment (or success) and incompletion as evidence of failure (p. 381-382)." In neither experiment were the characteristic differences in achievement motivation expressed in behavior when it had been made perfectly clear to subjects that task performance could not be considered a test of their ability.

What is different about the two studies? The difference, and it represents a very substantial advance in level of aspiration after twenty years, is that Weiner and others (Heckhausen, 1973) now seek to describe more fully the cognitions which intervene between antecedent instruction and consequent action. They seek, in brief, to give a full account of the meaning of the situation to the individual.

Motivation theory to be complete, however, must include both an account of the effects of antecedent conditions on the dispositions to action and an account of how these dispositions eventuate in action. With respect to the latter, we think the motivational processes set forth in the dynamics of action are promising and we are ever ready to look for their applicability to research findings generated by other notions. It is in this spirit, in order to illustrate how the dynamics of action can be used, that we comment in some detail on one of the papers of the symposium.

In "Cognitive Appraisals and Transformations in Self-Control," Professor Mischel confronts the problem of the regulation of overt activity by cognitive processes. He does so empirically, in a series of well-designed studies that convincingly demonstrate the determinative role of the content of consciousness in the motivation of action.

The method used in all the studies places a child in a situation where he is waiting for the experimenter to return in order to receive a preferred object (e.g., marshmallows), but where he can signal the experimenter to return and receive a less preferred object (e.g., pretzels). Mischel refers to this situation as one of "delay of gratification" and indicates that "waiting" is the subject of interest in his experiments. We agree that the activity of waiting is under study and would like to show how the dynamics of action can be employed in the theoretical analysis of some of his results.

"To wait," according to the dictionary, is "to remain inactive or stay in one spot until something anticipated occurs." The latter meaning seems entirely appropriate to Mischel's situations. In his first study (Mischel & Ebbesen, 1970), the child is instructed by the experimenter: "If you sit very still in your chair until I come back *by myself*, then you can eat the _____ [preferred reward]! (p. 332)." Thus, as the experimenter leaves the child alone in the room, the child's ongoing activity can be described as "waiting for the experimenter to return in order to receive the preferred object" or, more succinctly, as "waiting for the preferred object."

An alternative activity is also well defined for the child by the experimenter (Mischel & Ebbesen, 1970): "But if you want to make me come back all you have to do is press that [pointing to signal] and I'll come back; but then you can't have the _____ [preferred reward]; but you can have all the _____ [less preferred] (p. 332)." This alternative activity can be described as "signalling for the experimenter to return in order to receive the less preferred object" or "signalling for the less preferred object."

Basically, what is involved here is a change of activity. The child is engaged in the activity of "waiting for the preferred object" (Activity A) and, if a change of activity occurs within the time allotted, it is a change to the alternative activity of "signalling for the less preferred object" (Activity B). Using our notation, we have $T_{A_I} > T_{B_I}$ at the beginning of the interval of observation (when the experimenter leaves the room) and $T_{B_F} > T_{A_F}$ at some later point in time (when the child signals). Initially the tendency to "wait for the preferred object" is stronger than the tendency to "signal for the less preferred object," but subsequently the latter tendency dominates the former and the change of activity takes place. The time required for this change of activity to occur is both the latency of the signalling and the persistence of the waiting (called the "waiting period" by Mischel).

Analysis of this change of activity begins by coming to grips with the forces determining the strength of the competing tendencies. Looking first at the ongoing activity A, we note that as the child is "waiting for the preferred object" he is sitting still and *anticipating receiving the preferred object*. According to principles stated in the dynamics of action, as long as activity A continues T_A is subjected to both instigating *and* consummatory forces. As a consequence, the strength of T_A is moving toward its asymptote of F_A/c_A. During this same period of time, the tendency for activity B (signalling for the less preferred object) is being instigated but not consumed. It therefore grows in strength monotonically. Since activity B is not occurring, there can be no direct consummatory effect on T_B. For simplicity, we shall also assume that there is no substitution from the ongoing activity A to tendency B.[1]

Realistically, one must expect that the instigation and consummation of T_A are not continuous but intermittent during the interval of observation. Likewise, the instigation of T_B should also be intermittent rather than continuous. Mischel's observations that some children covered their eyes with their hands, rested their heads on their arms, talked quietly to themselves, created games with their hands and feet, etc., are certainly evidence that exposure to the forces is intermittent. Nevertheless, it is not unreasonable that the change of activity can be represented adequately by an idealized picture drawn as if exposure to the forces were continuous.

Here is how this works. During each interval of time in which activity A is occurring, T_A is approaching its asymptote, F_A/c_A. During those intervals in which activity A is not occurring, T_A remains unchanged.[2] Therefore, over time T_A is moving ever closer to F_A/c_A and how close T_A approaches this

---

[1] This assumption is probably not entirely correct since "waiting for the preferred object" and "signalling for the less preferred object" are based on the same activity (e.g., eating) and therefore could be expected to involve substitution. However, the magnitude of substitution should be small and the differences from one condition to another in Mischel's experiments are only slight.

[2] This assumption that T_A is instigated only when activity A is occurring follows from having defined waiting as involving thinking about the anticipated outcome. Thus, while sitting still, the child is "waiting" only while also anticipating the preferred object. This is also the time during which the instigation for the waiting activity occurs.

value is positively related to the amount of time during which Activity A is ongoing.

Instigation of activity B (signalling for the less preferred object) must also be variable. It is our position that the content of thought can instigate action, but we must assume a stream of thought varying in content. The upward path of the strength of T_B will be stepwise and can be approximated by a straight line.

Figure 1 presents a schematic representation of the paths of T_A and T_B. In order to keep things simple, we have not attempted to include tendencies for the other activities in the stream or to show the origins of the forces for T_A and T_B. As a first approximation, one can take the solid lines of Figure 1 to be the courses of T_A and T_B and from them obtain the equation for the time for a change of activity. This equation, $t_{B/A} = \left(T_{A_F} - T_{B_I}\right)/F_B$, is presented and discussed in our paper.

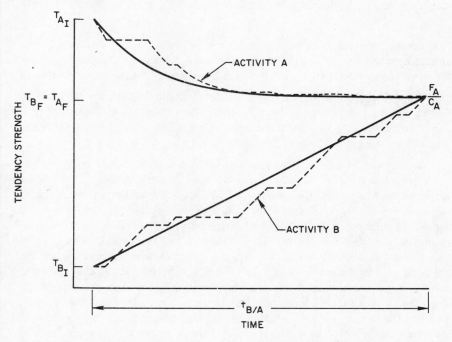

FIG. 1. *Continuous approximations to noncontinuous changes in the strengths of tendencies.*

With this basic analysis accomplished, we can address some of the specific and interesting results obtained by Mischel in his experiments. Consider the findings of Mischel and Ebbesen (1970) that the time for a change of activity is related to the physical presence and absence of the preferred and less preferred objects. The time taken to change from "waiting for the preferred object" to "signalling for the less preferred object" was greatest when neither object was present. The time was significantly shorter when either one of the objects was visible to the children and shortest when both objects were visible.

Let us allow the graph of Figure 1 to represent the time to change activity when neither object is present (i.e., the condition yielding the greatest time). It is apparent from the graph and from the equation for $t_{B/A}$ that all three variables (T_{A_F}, T_{B_I} and F_B) can affect the time for a change in activity. The greater the strength of tendency for activity A (T_{A_F}), the longer it will take for T_B to intercept it. The stronger the initial tendency for activity B (T_{B_I}), the less time it will take for T_B to reach T_A. The larger the instigating force for $T_B(F_B)$, the more rapid the increase in the strength of T_B and the sooner T_B will dominate T_A.

Let us now consider why the presence of only the less preferred object should decrease the waiting time (i.e., the time to initiate the signalling activity). Of the three variables, F_B seems the most likely source for the major portion of the effect. The sight of the less preferred object should instigate the tendency to "signal for the less preferred object," perhaps by increasing the amount of time the child thinks about having the less preferred object. This can be visualized in Figure 1 by imagining a steeper average slope for T_B.

In addition, it can be expected that instigation from the sight of the less preferred object to "signal for the less preferred object" (activity B) would be displaced to "waiting for the preferred object" (activity A). Displacement can be expected because the activities associated with the two objects are in the same family. "Waiting to eat cookies" and "signalling to eat pretzels," for example, should both be thought of as members of the "eating" family of activities.

If there is displacement from "signalling for the less preferred object" to "waiting for the preferred object" (i.e., from activity B to activity A), the child should spend more time thinking about "waiting" as well as thinking about "signalling" as compared to the condition in which neither object is physically present. The consequence of spending more time thinking about "waiting for the preferred object" is to move the tendency for that activity (T_A) even closer to its asymptote (F_A/c_A). This should have only a minor effect on the time to change activities because of the negatively accelerated path taken by T_A. As can be observed in Figure 1, changes in the strength of T_A with instigation are small once T_A gets close to its limiting value, F_A/c_A.

Mischel's finding that the presence of the preferred object also decreased the time required for a change of activity (i.e., resulted in quicker signalling for the less preferred object) can now be understood without introducing any new assumptions. First, the sight of the preferred object should provide direct instigation that increases the amount of time spent thinking about "waiting for the preferred object" (activity A). As a result, T_A approaches closer to F_A/c_A than when neither object is physically present. This alone, however, should not be expected to produce any major effect on the time to change activity, again because of the negatively accelerated path of T_A.

The second factor, displacement, appears to be more potent. Because they both belong to the same family of "eating" tendencies, the instigation from the sight of the preferred object should be displaced to the activity of "signalling for the less preferred object," increasing the overall instigation for that activity. The consequence of this is a more rapid growth in the strength of the tendency for the signalling activity and a shorter time for initiating that activity than in the case when neither object is present. The effect of displacement would appear in the equation for $t_{B/A}$ as a larger F_B. It can be visualized as a steeper slope for T_B in Figure 1.

Finally, in terms of the analysis already presented, the condition in which both the preferred and less preferred objects are in sight would be expected to produce the quickest change of activity. Under this condition direct instigation from the preferred object and displacement from the less preferred object combine to bring the tendency to "wait for the preferred object" toward asymptote, and direct instigation from the less preferred object and displacement from the preferred object combine to steepen the growth of the tendency to "signal for the less preferred object." The magnitude of these combined effects in reducing the waiting time can be expected to be greater than either of the separate effects.

Thus, the pattern of results from the four conditions in the Mischel and Ebbesen experiment can be interpreted and understood as examples of changes of activity under different conditions of direct and displaced instigation. If this interpretation of the results is theoretically sound, one would expect a much weaker effect of having the preferred object present when there is no less preferred object in the experiment at all. If the two activities of interest were "waiting for the preferred object" (activity A) versus merely "signalling for the presence of the experimenter" (activity B), for example, one might then expect little or no displacement between the two activities. This is because the two activities are no longer two instances of eating, i.e., members of the same family of tendencies. It would follow that now there should be no reduction in the time to change activity with the preferred object present as compared to the condition with no objects present.

The additional data Mischel reports in his paper are extensive and convincing in the story they tell. Even for a preschool child the content of thought (i.e., the content of the stream of covert activity) appears to be a powerful regulator of the overt activities of the child. It is difficult to avoid the conclusion (and we see no reason to do so) that instigation to action, and presumably inhibition of action, may originate in conscious thought. From the standpoint of the dynamics of action, the analysis of the stream of overt activity must include prior analysis of the stream of covert activity and its motivational significance.

In our paper we gave an account of how the dynamics of action can be extended to encompass the cognitive control of action simply by adopting the proposal that the content of thought can instigate action. This proposal allows us to utilize all the richness of the theory as it already exists. We undertook the analysis of a fictitious situation contrived to be a rather pure and fairly dramatic example of cognitive control of action. Little did we realize that Mischel and his associates have already made it possible to move that analysis from the fiction to the nonfiction shelf!

REFERENCES

Atkinson, J.W. The achievement motive and recall of interrupted and completed tasks. *Journal of Experimental Psychology*, 1953, *46*, 381-390.

Atkinson, J.W., & Birch, D. *The dynamics of action*. New York: John Wiley & Sons, 1970.

Atkinson, J.W., & Birch, D. The dynamics of achievement-oriented activity. In Atkinson, J.W. & Raynor, J.O. (Eds.) *Motivation and achievement*. Washington, D.C.: V.H. Winston, (Distributed by Halsted Press of John Wiley & Co.), 1974.

Birch, D. Shift in activity and the concept of persisting tendency. In Spence, K.W., & Spence, J.T. (Eds.) *The psychology of learning and motivation: Advances in research and theory, II*. New York: Academic Press, 1968.

Heckhausen, H. Intervening cognitions in motivation. In *Pleasure, reward, preference*. New York-London: Academic Press, 1973, pp. 217-242.

Jones, E.E., Rock, L., Shaver, K.G., Goethals, G.R., & Ward, L.M. Pattern of performance and ability attribution: An unexpected primacy effect. *Journal of Personality and Social Psychology*, 1968, *10*, 317-340.

Mischel, W., & Ebbesen, E.G. Attention in delay of gratification. *Journal of Personality and Social Psychology*, 1970, *16*, 329-337.

Raynor, J.O. Future orientations and motivation of immediate activity: An elaboration of the theory of achievement motivation. *Psychological Review*, 1969, *76*, 606-610. Reprinted with experiments and elaborations in Atkinson, J.W. & Raynor, J.O. (Eds.) *Motivation and achievement*. Washington, D.C.: V.H. Winston, (Distributed by Halsted Press of John Wiley & Co.), 1974.

Sears, R.R. A theoretical framework for personality and social behavior. *American Psychologist*, 1951, *9*, 476-483.

Comments on the Discussion

Bernard Weiner

University of California, Los Angeles

When arranging this symposium my deepest fear was that there would be four nonoverlapping research addresses. The symposium would then suffer the fate of too many other symposia, namely, a lack of focus and an absence of a harmony of ideas. But, to the contrary, a number of methodological and conceptual agreements emerged between the speakers.

Let me first address the methodological issue. There is a movement to consider more seriously the self-generated and naturally occurring behavior of individuals. For example, Lazarus is concerned with the coping strategies that individuals normally use to handle threat and to regulate their emotions. Mischel identifies the cognitive control mechanisms that children typically use to delay gratification. And my colleagues and I have identified the perceived causes of success and failure by establishing free-response situations in which individuals merely are asked to tell their causal beliefs. In sum, we are all guided by and moving toward the natural cognitive activities of the person (as Bolles also points out).

To identify these cognitive constructions, individuals often are asked to give reports about their mental (covert) activities. They are asked what do they ideate, what do they perceive, and so on. This methodology smacks of the long-forbidden introspective method, and Mischel is particularly careful not to fall into any traps. It is evident, then, that we need to develop sophisticated cognitive methodologies. We need to be able to discern what are these thoughts that are carried around and what are these transformational and construction processes. For Freud, the dream was the "royal road" to the unconscious. We need some royal roads to the conscious, roads that function as mental X-rays and serve as research superhighways.

The discussion of methodology brings me to a second point. Advances in psychology often are made when a reference experiment is devised. This is an experiment that demonstrates our position, that produces systematic and reliable data, that is amenable to different kinds of variations. It is the conditioning procedure of Pavlov, the instrumental learning procedure of Thorndike, the operant procedure of Skinner.

Reference experiments or procedures were well represented in this symposium. Mischel places children in a choice-delay setting. He can then partially influence what is thought during the delay interval. Lazarus shows his subjects stressful films. He can then partially influence what is thought during the film presentation. Both Mischel and Lazarus report systematic and reliable data utilizing a basic experimental procedure and variants of this procedure. They have found a paradigm that works and made a long-term commitment to it. Our attribution work makes use of two or three such reference experiments, manipulating the perceived causes of success and failure or inducing achievement outcomes and examining causal ascriptions.

Such a reference experiment is exactly what Birch, Atkinson and Bongort need to overcome the criticism leveled by Sears that their model is not tied to empirical data. Further, when Sears suggests that Mischel and I should expand our domains, he is asking us to leave the safety and warmth of our reference experiments and find some others. That often is difficult.

Now let me turn from methodology to some conceptual issues. The focus of the work of Lazarus, Mischel, and myself has been on internal acts rather than upon external stimuli. The implicit assumption in our work is that man is an active, construing organism rather than a passive, mechanistic being. The issues raised concern the always ongoing constructive processes rather than the objective, distal stimulus. We are indeed in the Diagram 6 stage, as depicted by Bolles.

It also is evident that we have been asking about the nature of ideation and how it affects action. And we have labeled some mental content as "good" or "bad." That is, it is intimated that some covert activity is better or more adaptive than others. For example, focusing upon the cue value of a stimulus rather than its motivational properties aids delay of gratification; using particular coping strategies during a stressful situation is ego-protective; and ascribing failure to a lack of effort rather than to a lack of ability promotes achievement striving. Delay strategies, ways of dealing with stress, and causal ascriptions are coping mechanisms.

It would appear, then, that we are cognitive functionalists, and we have been examining the relationships between covert activities and, if you will, survival. This is an evolutionary point of view that places the work reported in this volume within a broader scientific framework. It is evident that a cognitive functionalism is being developed that is every bit as precise and as scientific as behavioral functionalism, which is our recent heritage. It also is clear that humanistic conceptions of man can be accompanied by the scientific precepts so carefully nourished by the behaviorists and the neobehaviorists.

AUTHOR INDEX

A

Allport, G., 90
Armstrong, W., 63, 69
Atkinson, J. W., 13, 17, 20, 72, 78, 79,
84-87, 89, 91, 92, 98
Augustine, St., 3, 4
Averill, J. R., 21, 25, 26, 32

B

Baker, N., 44-46, 49
Bandura, A., 90
Bechterev, V. M., 8, 20
Berlyne, D., 43, 49
Birch, D., 17, 72, 75, 84-87, 89, 98, 100
Bolles, R. C., 7, 20, 85, 89, 90, 99
Bongort, K., 17, 85-87, 89, 100
Bowlby, J., 90

C

Cohen, F., 30, 32
Cook, R. E., 52, 56, 58, 59, 69
Curran, R. S., 22, 32
Currie, A. R., 22, 32

D

Davidson, J. N., 22, 32
Davison, L. A., 46, 49
Descartes, R., 72
Dollard, J., 87, 90
Dulany, D. E., Jr., 40, 49

E

Ebbesen, E. B., 35-37, 39-43, 49, 93, 94,
97, 98
Estes, W. K., 43, 49
Eswara, H. S., 63, 68

F

Fontaine, G., 56, 61, 68
Fox, R. S., 25, 27, 32
Freud, S., 6, 7, 10-12, 21, 32, 34, 41, 44,
49, 86, 89, 90, 99
Friedman, S. B., 25, 27, 32
Frieze, I., 52-54, 68, 69
Fuller, R., 63, 69

G

Gal, R., 31, 32
Goethals, G. R., 92, 98
Goldstein, M., 56, 59, 61, 68
Gray, S. J., 22, 32
Guthrie, E. R., 84

H

Hamilton, G. V., 86, 89
Harlow, H. F., 90
Heckhausen, H., 52, 56, 58, 59, 63, 68, 69,
92, 98
Heider, F., 18, 20, 51, 68
Hofer, M. A., 25, 27, 32
Hull, C. L., 7, 9, 10, 12, 13, 20, 72, 86, 89

J

James, W., 4
Jones, E. E., 98

K

Kaplan, R. M., 63, 68
Kelley, H. H., 53, 68
Koriat, A., 25, 26, 32
Krakaner, L. J., 22, 32
Kukla, A., 52-54, 62, 63, 68, 69
Kun, A., 53, 68

SUBJECT INDEX

A

Ability attributions, 52
  antecedents, 53
  related to affect, 63, 64
Active organism, 16-19, 73, 85, 100
Action tendency, 76, 77
Aesop's fable, 19
Arousal, 43, 48
Associationism, 7, 10
Attention, manipulation, 39
Autopsy, reactions, 25, 27

B

Behavioral change, 73-75, 77-81, 82, 93-95, 97
Black-box, 33, 85-88

C

Causal attributions, 18, 19, 23
  antecedents, 53-55, 87
  determinants of performance, 64-68
  and need achievement, 18
  related to affect, 61-67
  related to expectancy, 56-61, 65-67
  for success and failure, 51, 52
Causal biases, individual differences, 54
Causal dimensions, 52, 54, 55
Causal schemata, necessary causality, 53
  sufficient causality, 53
Causal stability, 52
  influence on expectancy, 56, 57, 59-61
Cognition, and achievement striving, 92
  defined, 85
  and emotion, 21
  related to action, 71, 72, 79, 80, 82-84, 86, 91
Cognitive appraisal, 15, 21-24, 46
Cognitive control, *see* Self-control

Cognitive functionalism, 100
Cognitive models, 13, 16
Cognitive psychology, 89, 90
  history, 1-5, 7, 11, 12, 14, 86
  scientific study, 86, 99
Cognitive transformation, 38, 44-48, 86, 89, 100
Competing tendencies, 94-96
Coping, 15, 21, 22, 24-30, 88
  anticipatory, 27
  individual differences, 31

D

Defense mechanism, 6, 15
  humor, 25
Delay of gratification, 17, 18, 34, 37-43, 45-48, 88, 93, 94, 96, 97
  and distraction, 38, 39, 41
  influenced by attention, 35, 36, 38, 41, 44
  and rewards, 44, 46
Delay strategies, 37
Denial, 15, 27
Detachment, 25, 26
Displacement, 96, 97
Drive, 9, 10, 13
Dynamics of action, 72, 75, 78-80, 91, 93, 98

E

Effort attributions, 52
  antecedents, 53
  related to affect, 63-68
Emotion, 4, 7, 15, 17, 21-27, 29, 31
  control of, 26
  influence of causal attribution, 61-68
  and performance, 65-67
Ethology, 16, 22
Expectancy, 11, 12, 52, 55

A 4
B 5
C 6
D 7
E 8
F 9
G 0
H 1
I 2
J 3